#FaithGoals

Petra Pindar

Petra Pindar, Inc Publishing
PO Box 358321
Gainesville, FL 32635

All rights reserved. No part of this book may be reproduced, transmitted, decompiled, reverse engineered or stored in or introduced into any information storage retrieval in any form or by any means, whether electronic, or mechanical, now known or hereinafter invented with the expressed written permission of the publisher, Petra Pindar, Inc Publishing.

Scripture quotations identified KJV are from the authorized King James Version. Rights in the authorized version in the United Kingdom are vested in the Crown. Reproduced by permission of the Crown's patentee, Cambridge University Press.

Scripture quotations identified NKJV are from the New King James Version ®. Copyright © 1982 by Thomas Nelson. Used by permission. All rights reserved.

Scripture quotations identified NIV are from The Holy Bible, New International ®, NIV ® Copyright © 1973, 1978, 1984, 2011 by Biblica, Inc. ® Used by permission. All rights reserved worldwide.

Scripture quotations marked CSB have been taken from the Christian Standard Bible ®, Copyright © 2017 by Holman Bible Publishers. Used by permission. Christian Standard Bible•, and CSB® are federally registered trademarks of Holman Bible Publishers.

Scripture quotations marked ESV are from the ESV® Bible (The Holy Bible, English Standard Version®), copyright© 2001 by Crossway Bibles, a publishing ministry of Good News Publishers. Used by permission. All rights reserved.

Copyright © 2019

Photography by Stacey Muniz

All rights reserved, including the right to reproduce this book or portions thereof in any form whatsoever.

Dedicated to my babies. Jackson and Sterling, you have changed my life in a way that solidifies my faith. I love you.

Contents

Foreword by *Brelyn Bowman* vii
Introduction 1

Persistent Faith 3
    Delayed NOT Denied 7
    Distance Makes the Heart Grow Fonder 13
    The Perspective of Promise 19
    Undeterred 27
    Promise Fulfilled 31
    Week 1 Exercise 37

Faith in Battle 39
    Line in the Sand 43
    Love Freely Given 53
    Go Anyway 59
    Your End = His Beginning 67
    Go the Distance 73
    Week 2 Exercise 79

Restorative Faith 81
    Broken Not Worthless 85
    Unlikely Protection 91
    Covered 95
    There is Still Time 101
    Stick to the Plan 105
    Week 3 Exercise 109

Courageous Faith 113
    Peace Be Still 117
    Eyes on the Prize 125
    Don't Give Up the Pursuit 131
    Pre-Planned 137
    Pursuit of Faith 141
    Week 4 Exercise 145

Epilogue 147
About The Author 149

Foreword by *Brelyn Bowman*

From the moment I met Petra, I knew she was a strong woman. One who doesn't quit in the face of adversity and one that doesn't back down when people say she can't. Petra's heart at the core is to see women live out their God ordained assignments. She wants to fortify women by letting them know that they too can fight the good fight. In this four-week roadmap, Petra encourages you to go after God and start a relationship with Him. She shares how many have lost that time with Him and how she rediscovered the beauty of having a meaningful relationship with the Father. I share the desire for women to have a relationship with God that will inspire others. I pray that you enjoy this journey she takes you on but not just for your enjoyment, but to take it to other women to inspire them to build a meaningful relationship too.

God Bless,

Brelyn Bowman

INTRODUCTION

It's 1:26am on October 13, 2017. I'm literally crying as my little family sleeps. I had no idea that I'd lost faith in Him. While sharing Him, while worshipping Him, while serving Him. While loving Him. I forgot who He is. For months my heart has gotten heavier and heavier, with no explanation. And it's odd because this year I stepped out on faith and began to build the community I have always been passionate about. Perhaps even as a child. And yet, I am not happy. Because I have lost sight of Him. I must share some things with you. Before I lose the words. Before I lose the nerve. For I have come to realize that we must actively pursue joy in the process of growing our faith.

What's beautiful, is that I have found that there are so many of you who are navigating your faith. I am honored to share some of your stories. I am also excited to share the stories of Biblical women who solidified their faith and attained fulfillment in Him. My prayer is that this compilation of stories provides a road map to healing, clarity and forgiveness. For yourself. For others. And even our misplaced anger towards God when we thought He had forgotten us. Because there is certainly anger.

But even in your anger, I encourage you to remember that there is no love quite like His. His love is perfect. In every way. It is designed to pursue you even when you are running or feel undesirable. It is relentless and unyielding. His love will never grow tired of you or turn from fighting for you. His love will fulfill and satisfy in ways that no person ever could. There is no comparison to the way that He chooses to love you.

His love is extraordinary, unending, immeasurable and intentional. There is nothing that His love cannot cover if you allow it to.

Romans 8:38-39 *For I am convinced that neither death nor life, neither angels nor demons, neither the present nor the future, nor any powers, neither height nor depth, nor anything else in all creation, will be able to separate us from the love of God that is in Christ Jesus our Lord. (NIV)*

All He requires is that we have faith the size of a mustard seed. Faith can be messy, complicated, and heavy. The goal is to find joy and purpose in the process… Even when we don't feel happy or sure. #faithgoals

*Note: some names have been changed to protect the privacy of the women sharing their stories and their supportive families. Their stories have also been edited by my words to capture the spirit of their thoughts.

Week 1

Persistent Faith

This week we are going to focus on the blessing within having persistent faith. Not only is God persistently pursuing you, He wants you to pursue Him. It is vital for us to learn that having a level of persistent faith factors into receiving the promise.

There is this strange idea, that you don't have to put in any type of work to receive. But if you're willing to work for a paycheck on your regular job why are we not as consistent in pursuing the promises of God? There are so many instances in the Word where because of someone's persistence God *favored* them and God showed them that their persistence was the key. So, this next story I hope will open your eyes to the reality that there has to be persistent pursuit of the promise.

Monet and her beautiful family are first. Their story is one that will allow you to look past your personal hopes and into God's purpose. And love, that's important because your hopes are not always the end goal, but they can propel us towards the purpose that has been planned for us.

Then I want to share with you the stories of four women who defied the odds and continued to pursue the presence of God even when it seemed silly. And can I tell you a secret? Most times, it will seem silly to keep pushing and activating your faith. I encourage you to do it anyway. It's not about the naysayers it is about the One who knew the answer before the question was ever asked.

If you need additional support, check out the memory verses for this week!

1 Corinthians 1:25 *Because God's foolishness is wiser than human wisdom, and God's weakness is stronger than human strength.* (CSB)

1 Corinthians 1:18 *For the word of the cross is foolishness to those who are perishing, but it is the power of God to us who are being saved.* (CSB)

1 Corinthians 2:14 *But the person without the Spirit does not receive what comes from God's Spirit, because it is foolishness to him; he is not able to understand it since it is evaluated spiritually. (CSB)*

It is important to read and memorize these verses as a reminder that even when it may seem like foolishness, it falls within His plan perfectly.

Day 1
Delayed NOT Denied

MONET

When Monet first reached out to me, I had no idea that her story would be one of restoration and hope. Restoration of faith, of peace, of understanding and of relationship. As we chatted on the phone, immediately the below scripture dropped into my spirit.

Isaiah 61:7 *Instead of your shame you will receive a double portion, and instead of disgrace you will rejoice in your inheritance. And so you will inherit a double portion in your land, and everlasting joy will be yours. (NIV)*

I hope that you will hear Monet's story with your heart as one that is a necessary conversation for so many women…so many families.

Here's Monet.

Let me start by saying that I feel passionately about infertility and the necessity to communicate with your circle. You never know who is going through something similar or who needs to hear your story of faith.

My faith was built as we struggled with infertility for the first 5 years of our marriage.

As a teenager I was told that I might not be able to have children. It wasn't that it was confirmed that I could NOT get pregnant but that it may be difficult for me to become pregnant. But I wouldn't know for sure until I tried to have children.

However, I knew that God had shown me that I would have children. Likewise, my husband was also told by God that he would be surrounded by children. Little did I know that God had separately planted these seeds in our hearts to keep us encouraged. It is so important to remember that there is a process to manifestation and the seed is only a small portion of that greater process.

When my husband and I decided to try, we quickly realized that we couldn't become pregnant. After a year of trying we began to see a specialist. That began our long process of trying different methods to increase our fertility chances. It is important to realize that sometimes God will show us the outcome but will keep the path hidden. We had to trust in the Word that He has given us and the reality that His promises are yes and amen and they are not predicated on how He did something for someone else.

Isaiah 43:19 *Behold, I will do a new thing; now it shall spring forth; shall ye not know it? I will even make a way in the wilderness, and rivers in the desert. (KJV)*

We finally became pregnant after opting to go the route of intrauterine insemination (IUI). It was hard because we felt like there were no other black or minority couples who were going through this process. To be frank, we didn't think that we had any FRIENDS who were going through this process. Or at least no friends who were talking about it. But in this season of isolation, we leaned further into our belief that God would follow through. We became pregnant the first time doing IUI. In fact, we became pregnant with quadruplets. Unfortunately, we lost one but the remaining three were born healthy. Two girls and a boy.

TAKEAWAY LESSON

Through the persistent pursuit of the fulfillment of what God told Monet and her husband, they experienced the promise. Don't get weary in well-doing. And well-doing surely encompasses bringing God glory through the fulfillment of His promises.

Begin to meditate on the below scripture bank to begin to renew your mind towards Him and His promises. You'll notice that He will tell you the "what" but He will not always tell you "how" and I want you to rest in the beauty of not having to plan but just follow His lead.

We have grown so accustomed to the need to plan our lives out to the last detail that we have forgotten that we are not the creators of our lives in the first place. It is time that we give Him the opportunity to be God and ourselves the grace to be humans in need of a divine appointment.

SCRIPTURE BANK

Jeremiah 17:14 *Heal me, LORD, and I will be healed; save me and I will be saved, for you are the one I praise. (NIV)*

Jeremiah 29:11 *For I know the plans I have for you," declares the LORD, "plans to prosper you and not to harm you, plans to give you hope and a future. (NIV)*

1 John 5:4 *for everyone born of God overcomes the world. This is the victory that has overcome the world, even our faith. (NIV)*

1 Peter 5:10 *And the God of all grace, who called you to his eternal glory in Christ, after you have suffered a little while, will himself restore you and make you strong, firm and steadfast. (NIV)*

John 14:1 *Do not let your hearts be troubled. You believe in God; believe also in me. (NIV)*

Zechariah 9:12 *Return to your fortress, you prisoners of hope; even now I announce that I will restore twice as much to you. (NIV)*

Psalm 71:20-21 **20** *Though you have made me see troubles, many and bitter, you will restore my life again; from the depths of the earth you will again bring me up.* **21** *You will increase my honor and comfort me once more. (NIV)*

2 Corinthians 13:9-11 **9** *We are glad whenever we are weak, but you are strong; and our prayer is that you may be fully restored.* **10** *This is why I write these things when I am absent, that when I come I may not have to be harsh in my use of authority—the authority the Lord gave me for building you up, not for tearing you down.* **11** *Finally, brothers and sisters, rejoice! Strive for full restoration, encourage one another, be of one mind, live in peace. And the God of love and peace will be with you. (NIV)*

Proverbs 3: 5-6 *Trust in the Lord with all thine heart; and lean not unto thine own understanding. In all thy ways acknowledge him, and he shall direct thy paths. (KJV)*

Psalm 31: 24 *Be of good courage, and he shall strengthen your heart, all ye that hope in the Lord. (KJV)*

Psalm 113:9 *He maketh the barren woman to keep house, and to be a joyful mother of children. Praise ye the Lord. (KJV)*

PRAYER OF COURAGE

Father God, in the name of Jesus, thank you. Thank you for courage. Thank you for the ability to lean into you and press forward, even when the path is daunting. Thank you for opening our eyes to your hand in all things. Thank you for the courage not to stay discouraged. Thank you for the wisdom of knowing that you will do a new thing in us. There are unconventional miracles that you have set aside for us. We just have to trust your plan. Thank you for being bigger than our fears. Our courage comes from the reality of your goodness. You have never failed… and you won't start now. In Jesus' name, amen.

Day 2
Distance Makes the Heart Grow Fonder

"Bloody, yet unbowed." -Invictus

THE WOMAN WITH THE ISSUE OF BLOOD

I am sure that many of you have heard of the woman with the issue of blood. The disease that paralyzed her for 12 years. If not, I encourage you to read about her in Matthew 9:20-22, Mark 5: 25-34 and Luke 8:43- 48. Her story will shake you to your core, especially if you find a seven-day cycle to be debilitating.

But what I absolutely love about her story is that there was no-one who could heal her. There was nothing about her that was redeeming. I know that we all can relate to the feeling of complete brokenness and exhaustion. The Bible talks about how she was ostracized, and I would venture incredibly undesirable. I imagine that she was painfully and overwhelmingly exhausted by the futile attempts to end her discomfort and loss of life. Yet, she never gave up. That will preach all by itself. She. Never. Gave. Up. And let's be clear, she had every right to do so.

I dare say that there are some of you that are currently in the same position of discomfort. You have tried every resource available to you and nothing has worked. And you have one last option in your pocket. But it's a long shot. Take the shot, love bug. This woman was down to her last option and she refused to miss the opportunity to put it into action.

When she heard about Jesus coming into town, she made sure that she was in the area and fought her way to get close enough to touch him. She pushed through the throngs of people that surrounded Him and seemingly barred her path to freedom. It wasn't about if He made deliberate contact, it was about if SHE did. She was determined that the promises of God concerning her would be fulfilled and nothing would stand in her way. She knew that He was able to heal her, without any special prayer or acknowledgement. She just had to have the faith to propel His action. I like to think that even now, if we choose to just trust Him, He will do the rest. You just have to get close enough. You have to pursue Him. You must touch the hem of His garment, by any means necessary. Don't get distracted.

When we get past the place of thinking that He has to do things on our timeline and the way that we desire, we will begin to properly position ourselves in His path and within His plan. It's not going to always be a glamorous encounter, but it can be a victorious testimony. Once we have to come to the understanding that His glory is predicated on His adherence to His Word and His promises, we will worry less and will focus more on proper positioning. Distance does not mean that He cannot feel us or address our needs. It is just His way of pushing us to be more intentional in our pursuit and committed to the process of investing in our own growth.

AFFIRMATIONS

He has not forgotten me.

He has not failed me.

The anointing that is in Him, rests on me.

SCRIPTURE BANK

Psalms 145:14-16 **14** *The Lord upholds all who fall and lifts up all who are bowed down.* **15** *The eyes of all look to you, and you give them their food at the proper time.* **16** *You open your hand and satisfy the desires of every living thing.* *(NIV)*

1 John 5:14-15 **14** *And this is the confidence that we have in him, that, if we ask any thing according to his will, he heareth us:* **15** *And if we know that he hear us, whatsoever we ask, we know that we have the petitions that we desired of him.* *(KJV)*

Psalm 71:20-21 **20** *Though you have made me see troubles, many and bitter, you will restore my life again; from the depths of the earth you will again bring me up.* **21** *You will increase my honor and comfort me once more.* *(NIV)*

Joel 2:25-26 **25** *"I will repay you for the years the locusts have eaten— the great locust and the young locust, the other locusts and the locust swarm — my great army that I sent among you.* **26** *You will have plenty to eat, until you are full, and you will praise the name of the LORD your God, who has worked wonders for you; never again will my people be shamed.* *(NIV)*

Jeremiah 30:17 *But I will restore you to health and heal your wounds,' declares the LORD, 'because you are called an outcast, Zion for whom no one cares.' (NIV)*

PRAYER OF HEALING

Father God, in the mighty name of Jesus. Thank you for another day to honor you and to bring glory to your name through my actions. Thank you for another opportunity to acknowledge your wisdom in all things concerning me. Even during my quiet season. Thank you for opening my eyes to the necessity of positioning myself to be healed through my active faith. Thank you for honoring my submission to your timeline and my desire to be at full capacity as I live my life for you. I don't ask for healing because I know that it is already done. I ask that you give me the proper mindset on how to maintain a healed body and mind so that I may continue to do the work that you have set before me. In Jesus' name, amen.

Day 3
The Perspective of Promise

HANNAH AND PENINNAH

I have a sneaking suspicion that you assumed this story would be first. And I can't blame you. Hannah has one of the most recognizable stories of barrenness in the Bible. But she also has one of the greatest stories of the stripping away of our personal desires to give room for His ultimate plan. She had to get past the place of wanting a child to prove her worth to society and enter into the mindset that everything that would come through her, ultimately belonged to God and should be used as He sees fit.

Go ahead and turn to 1 Samuel 1:2 and read all the way through 1 Samuel 2:21.

Okay, so now that you have gotten caught up on the drama between Hannah and Peninnah, let me share a few key things with you.

1. Stop worrying about what God is doing for the woman next to you. Begin to thank Him for the abundance of favor that pours out from her, that it begins to flood and overflow *your* space.

2. It's not about how people treat you, it's about how you treat them.

3. Just because society and social media have paraded certain ideals and goals, that doesn't mean that you must aspire to them. What God has for you supersedes what they have projected onto you.

4. Your promise has perspective. Once you shift from "mine" to "His", you will begin to see a shift in your prayers and therefore a shift in the way that you communicate your expectations of relationship with God.

Hannah was so distraught over not being able to have a child that she began to weep and essentially fall out before the Lord. However, in this place of despair she began to share with God that if He answered her prayer with a son, she would give the son to God for the rest of His life. I don't know about you, but that is mind blowing as a mother. To be given a child only to have to leave him in the care of another. I get that she was technically saying that she would leave him with God, but still! Hannah tapped into the idea that the promises concerning us are not always about us. In fact, her son Samuel would go on to be one of the greatest prophets in the Bible. His birth was a catalyst to turn the people back to God and to ensure the bloodline of Jesus. Talk about huge. But Hannah had to shift from thinking about having a child to bring her peace, to birthing a child to effectuate God's glory.

After Hannah conceived and gave birth to Samuel, she kept her word and returned Samuel to the temple of the Lord after he was weaned. I cannot imagine the pain that she must have felt to leave her small son in the care of Eli. But there is no reference to her hesitating or regretting her decision. In fact, in 1 Samuel 2: 1-10 she lifts a victorious prayer *thanking* God for His provision. Her perspective of the fulfilment of His promise had irrevocably shifted. And that's where we need to be. Get comfortable not understanding the level of investment that He requires. Because you are going to have to give up something and it may very well be the thing that He promised you.

But sweet friend, even in your sacrifice He is working behind the scenes for your good. As Samuel grew, Hannah and her husband would still come to the temple yearly to make a sacrifice to the Lord. And each year, Eli would pray this simple prayer, "May the Lord give you children by this woman in place of the one she has given to the Lord." God not only heard Eli's prayer, but He paid attention to Hannah's need and gave her three sons and two daughters. And not once did Hannah seek to remove Samuel from the temple as she waited for God to give her other children. There are three lessons there: 1) surround yourself with people that will continue to hold you accountable to God, 2) seek out covering that will not only pray God's blessings over you but your household, and 3) it can take years for the promise to manifest but your perspective has to be on the long-term goal and not the short-term gratification.

Hannah believed in the power of God even when it didn't appear that He intended to use it on her behalf. She prayed anyway asking boldly for her heart's desire. She trusted that He was a god of His word and in faith she dedicated a son that she *did not have* back to Him. Hannah's perspective was on the long-term goal of the promise. What's your perspective?

Now, let me share this last tidbit with you. Hannah initially got so caught up in Peninnah's taunts that she was not able to fully enjoy her husband, heed his advice to live a full life and bask in his adoration. Even childless, Elkanah would give Hannah a double portion and hold her in high regard over the wife who had borne him many children. Married friends, build a meaningful relationship with your husband and do not burden your marriage with the doubt and deceit of the world, that you are not enough. Build it up with the mentality to please God with all that you have…and all that you have yet to achieve. There is glory after this.

AFFIRMATIONS

What is in me will change the world.

There is glory in my waiting season.

My heartbreak does not lessen the majesty of God.

SCRIPTURE BANK

John 14:1 *"Do not let your hearts be troubled. You believe in God; believe also in me. (NIV)*

Mark 11:24 *Therefore I tell you, whatever you ask for in prayer, believe that you have received it, and it will be yours. (NIV)*

Matthew 6:33 *But seek first his kingdom and his righteousness, and all these things will be given to you as well. (NKJV)*

Psalm 23 **1** *The LORD is my shepherd, I lack nothing.* **2** *He makes me lie down in green pastures, he leads me beside quiet waters,* **3** *he refreshes my soul. He guides me along the right path for his name's sake.* **4** *Even though I walk through the darkest valley, I will fear no evil, for you are with me; your rod and your staff, they comfort me.* **5** *You prepare a table before me in the presence of my enemies. You anoint my head with oil; my cup overflows.* **6** *Surely your goodness and love will follow me all the days of my life, and I will dwell in the house of the LORD forever. (NIV)*

Psalm 51:12 **12** *Restore to me the joy of your salvation and grant me a willing spirit, to sustain me. (NIV)*

Psalm 71:20-21 **20** *Though you have made me see troubles, many and bitter, you will restore my life again; from the depths of the earth you will again bring me up.* **21** *You will increase my honor and comfort me once more. (NIV)*

Psalm 119:36 *Incline my heart unto thy testimonies, and not to covetousness. (KJV)*

Jeremiah 29: 12-13 **12** *Then you will call on me and come and pray to me, and I will listen to you.* **13** *You will seek me and find me when you seek me with all your heart. (NIV)*

PRAYER OF VICTORY

Father God, in the mighty name of Jesus. We are excited to come before you to bless you for the victory that is already won. We are honored to have the opportunity to showcase your goodness to all the earth. We are thankful for the strength that you are building in us as we wait to hear from you. Lord open our hearts and our minds to you and your will. Help us to hear your voice clearly so that we may know when to move and when to stand still. Help us to stay in position as you determine the next point of attack on the battlefield. Thank you for giving us grace when we forget that the victory is already won. In Jesus' name, amen.

Day 4
Undeterred

THE PARABLE OF THE PERSISTENT WIDOW

I'm going to throw you for a quick loop and share with you a quick parable found in Luke 18:1-8. And I say that because this story is not about someone who feared God, but it is instead about a judge who did not fear man *or* God. And yet, Jesus used this story to impress upon us the need to always pray and never give up.

In this short text, a widow who had nothing and no-one to speak for her, kept going to this judge requesting that he give her justice against her enemy. The judge wasn't moved. At first. But she *kept coming back* and would give him no peace. To be rid of her, he finally acknowledged and answered her need for justice.

The important part is that she never gave up. She kept coming back until he finally listened to her. I love that in verse 7 and 8a it says, *7 And will not God bring about justice for his chosen ones, who cry out to him day and night? Will he keep putting them off? 8 I tell you, he will see that they get justice, and quickly. (NIV)*

If a man who cared nothing about the widow and her actual needs could be moved to intercede on her behalf based on her persistence; it stands to reason that God will do the same for us. He just wants to see our consistency. It shouldn't be a whim that brings us into the presence of God, it should be a burning desire that we cannot contain that keeps us coming back. A desire to see Him for who He is. The Alpha and Omega.

When we constantly remind God of His word concerning us, He has to move. He *wants* to move. Do not lose focus and don't allow anything to deter you from what is rightfully yours.

AFFIRMATIONS

My blessing will make room for me.

I will see the end glory.

Giving up is not an option.

SCRIPTURE BANK

Psalms 9:10 *Those who know your name trust in you, for you, Lord, have never forsaken those who seek you. (NIV)*

Psalm 119:2 *Blessed are they that keep his testimonies, and that seek him with the whole heart. (NKJV)*

Psalm 119:11 *Thy word have I hid in mine heart, that I might not sin against thee. (KJV)*

Psalm 20:4 *May he give you the desire of your heart and make all your plans succeed. (NIV)*

Psalm 31: 24 *Be of good courage, and he shall strengthen your heart, all ye that hope in the Lord. (KJV)*

Proverbs 13:12 *Hope deferred maketh the heart sick: but when the desire cometh, it is a tree of life. (KJV)*

PRAYER OF PERSISTENCE

Father God, in the name of Jesus, thank you. Thank you for the opportunity to be in your presence and to experience another level of your glory. Right now, I also want to thank you for a heart to pursue and to not give up. Give me the mentality of Jacob in Genesis 32 that I will not let go until I receive your blessing and rename me according to my tenacity to never give up. I know that you are serious about me and my part in your greater plan. Keep my eyes focused on you and your path. All of my needs will be added accordingly. In Jesus' name, amen.

Day 5
Promise Fulfilled

SARAI/SARAH

You cannot rush God. Ever. And yet, we have an insatiable desire to help God pick up the pace when it comes to fulfilling His word. Why is that? It's not like we have anywhere else to be outside of His will. We have no great game plan outside of bringing Him glory. We have no desire that He has not met, at the right time. So why do we hurry God? Better question, why do we doubt God?

Every time I read the story of Sarah; I have these questions. She had seen firsthand the provision of God and yet she doubted His ability to give her a child in her old age. Ma'am. He created heaven and earth and all that dwells therein. Are you sure that you want to doubt that He can give you a child? Right. But she did. And we do. Often. That's why I couldn't finish this week without sharing Sarai's story and her journey to becoming Sarah.

Sarah was married to Abraham (formerly Abram) whom God had chosen to be the Father of a great nation. God's chosen people. (Genesis 17:1-8) But Sarah was ninety years old and barren. That didn't faze God at all. Read Genesis 17:15-16. God is not bothered by or bound to our ideas of what is possible. He creates, He restores, and He removes as He sees fit. It is time for us to embrace this truth just as Sarah had to in Genesis 18:14.

Unfortunately, before Sarah could rest in the knowledge of God's sovereignty, she got anxious. So anxious that she tells her husband to sleep with the handmaiden, Hagar, so that he will have a child. You read that right. Sarah became so anxious that she told her husband to sleep with someone else…and have a child. Read Genesis 16 for the entire story. But I want to point out the lesson: 1) don't get so anxious that you begin to work a plan that God never intended, 2) don't pull other people into your chaos because your trust has lost focus, and 3) don't create soul ties with people that you are only meant to disciple.

Now go ahead and read Genesis 21:1-7. God showed out. Abraham was one hundred years old and Sarah was ninety-one years old when their son Isaac was born. Neither of them understood the timeline of God but that did not change God's plan. Oftentimes, God will orchestrate a series of events to ensure that no-one else can get the credit for the outcome. He doesn't share the spotlight and He will not conform to what we think makes sense.

Isaiah 55:8-9 *8 For my thoughts are not your thoughts, neither are your ways my ways, saith the Lord. 9 For as the heavens are higher than the earth, so are my ways higher than your ways, and my thoughts than your thoughts. (KJV)*

What I want you to take away from Sarah's story is this; you can't hurry God and you can't beat Him at being God. Stop trying. There are better things to do with your time, like doing what you can with what He has already given you. His promise will be fulfilled, you just have to continue to move forward as if it is already done.

AFFIRMATIONS

His timing for my life is perfect.

There is nothing that He will withhold from me, in His will.

A delayed promise is not an unfulfilled promise.

SCRIPTURE BANK

Joshua 23:14 *And, behold, this day I am going the way of all the earth: and ye know in all your hearts and in all your souls, that not one thing hath failed of all the good things which the Lord your God spake concerning you; all are come to pass unto you, and not one thing hath failed thereof. (KJV)*

Isaiah 26:3 *Thou wilt keep him in perfect peace, whose mind is stayed on thee: because he trusteth in thee. (KJV)*

Isaiah 55:11 *So shall my word be that goeth forth out of my mouth: it shall not return unto me void, but it shall accomplish that which I please, and it shall prosper in the thing whereto I sent it. (KJV)*

2 Peter 3:9 *The Lord is not slack concerning his promise, as some men count slackness; but is longsuffering to us-ward, not willing that any should perish, but that all should come to repentance. (KJV)*

Philippians 4:7 *And the peace of God, which surpasses all understanding, will guard your hearts and your minds in Christ Jesus. (KJV)*

PRAYER OF PEACE

Father God, in the name of Jesus. Thank you for peace and for covering. You are not slack in your promises concerning us and you desire that we have fullness of joy, in you. Thank you for the peace that you desire to give to us as we pursue you and your will for our lives. Thank you for sending the Comforter to us, to relax our hearts as we wait to hear from you. Lord, we are thankful for this season of stretching and re-working. We take comfort in the knowledge that you would never leave us nor forsake us and that when we cannot understand the process, you have already determined the end. Thank you for the peace that surpasses all understanding. In Jesus' name, amen.

*Thank you for peace
and for covering.*

Week One Exercise

Today is the day to bare your soul. Pull the sheet from the mirror. Turn off the noise. Now, take out a piece of paper and write down every area that you have not trusted Him to heal. Every area that you are holding onto for fear it will be too much if anyone knew. Put down all the little things that have created a gaping hole in your heart. Write it all. Hold nothing back.

I mean it. Don't hold anything back. I don't care how messy, uncomfortable, embarrassing, heavy or bloody it is. I'm willing to guess that nothing you write down is a surprise to Him. Nothing.

Now, tear up your list. Burn it up. Flush it down the toilet. You choose how to annihilate your grief. Just get rid of it. Give it no way of escape. Don't re-read it again either. Just let it go.

1 Peter 5:7 *Casting all your cares on him, because he cares about you. (CSB)*

Too often we will lay an issue at His feet but will essentially pick it back up by re-reading or thinking about it. We don't truly trust Him to handle it or even understand it. I encourage you to give Him the room to show His hand to you through His ability to heal.

I am prayerful that your heart has now begun to beat a little slower and that your shoulders have lifted, ever so slightly. Good. Now, repeat after me… "He wants the best for me."

For the next 24 hours I want you to read, meditate, pray and rest in the following truths:

- You were created with purpose. That includes your scars and imperfections. Pursue it. Isaiah 43:6-7; 1 Corinthians 10:31; Matthew 5:16

- You are not alone. He has never forsaken you, beloved. Deuteronomy 31:6; Matthew 28:20; Romans 8:31-38

- You are not forgotten. His promises stand, even when we have fallen. 2 Corinthians 1:20

- You are worth the search. Just as you desire Him, He desires you. He's coming. 1 Samuel 12:22

During this time, every time a negative thought tries to distract you, speak one (or all!) of these affirmations over yourself. Don't give it any room to grow. Remind yourself of who you are and whose you are. If you constantly feed your mind peace, you will know peace.

If you realize that there are specific places or people that feed you toxicity, decide to cut ties and distance yourself. No second guessing. If there is ever a time that we are called to be bold in our love; it is to honor what He has created and not allow anything to pollute the temple of our bodies.

1 Kings 18:21 *Then Elijah approached all the people and said, "How long will you waver between two opinions? If the Lord is God, follow him. But if Baal, follow him." But the people didn't answer him a word. (CSB)*

You've got this, love. WE have got this.

Week 2

Faith in Battle

I am so excited about this week! We are learning battle strategy and how to see our victory through the chaos. Love bugs, it is so important for us to learn that there is going to be resistance from the enemy as we pursue Christ. He's not going to just let you go. Period. He's going to walk right up into your camp and pretend to be an ally. He's going to sow discord and dissension. Then he will nurture doubt and unbelief. And once he has confused your mind, dismantled your troops (friends) and annihilated your courage; he will draw you outside the boundaries of your camp. And that is the worst place to be.

Let the stories and lessons this week, build up your hedge of protection. Get comfortable ignoring the taunts of others and dodging the arrows of the enemy. We go through things to grow. Remember that. Every seedling had to push *through* the earth to reach towards the sun. Even when you must fight… push forward. He is pushing to get to you, too.

Your memory verses for this week:

Isaiah 12:2 *Indeed, God is my salvation; I will trust him and not be afraid, for the Lord, the Lord himself, is my strength and my song. He has become my salvation. (CSB)*

John 16:33 *I have told you these things, so that in me you may have peace. In this world you will have trouble. But take heart! I have overcome the world. (CSB)*

Revelation 12:11 *And they have conquered him by the blood of the Lamb and by the word of their testimony, for they loved not their lives even unto death. (ESV)*

Deuteronomy 3:22 *Don't be afraid of them, for the Lord your God fights for you. (CSB)*

Day 1
Line in the Sand

MECHELLE

When I read Mechelle's story, I immediately identified with her. Not because our stories are the same, but our brokenness was. I could easily hear the taunts and feel the dejection from my childhood, as I read her words. But what I love about her story is that it is the epitome of one of my favorite verses:

Isaiah 61:3 *To appoint unto them that mourn in Zion, to give unto them beauty for ashes, the oil of joy for mourning, the garment of praise for the spirit of heaviness; that they might be called trees of righteousness, the planting of the Lord, that he might be glorified. (KJV)*

As you read her story, I want you to reach way down and address those broken areas inside of you that you have hidden away. Bring them into the light and lay them on the altar.

Here's Mechelle.

Growing up I never understood why I was set up to fail within society. Wait, let me backtrack. I had an amazing childhood. No, it wasn't perfect, but I was loved, taken care of, and had all the normal childhood things that make childhood, a childhood. I guess not all good things last forever.

From head start until I was in third grade, I went to an elementary school that was a good mix of cultures but mostly "suburban". When I started fourth grade we moved, so I had to start riding the bus to get to my new school. This school was still a good mix of cultures but was mostly "urban" and I only knew one person, my sister. That bus is where I encountered my first "bully". I can remember it like it was yesterday, the first thing she ever said to me was "giving" me the nickname "burnt biscuit". I had never been taught to care about skin tones, complexions or anything of that nature. This was one of the most unnerving and gut-wrenching encounters, I have ever experienced. In my little world, if you were nice and I liked you, we were friends and that was it. I quickly learned that everyone wasn't like that. Or even close.

In that moment, I became aware and, ultimately, self-conscious of myself, my skin tone and my looks. I literally would try and hide or make myself as unnoticeable as possible. If there was nothing to see, there was nothing to pick on. Do you know how terrifying it is to feel trapped within a body that people poke at or make fun of and there is nothing that you can do?

Going into middle school all of the friends that I made the last two years of elementary school, ended up at a different middle school, so yay me, I had to start all over again. Sixth grade wasn't too bad. Of course, I still had encounters of bullies, but it was still a good year. Seventh grade was also a good year. Eighth grade was pretty good too, but eighth grade was also a year where another thing was brought to the forefront. My teeth.

As a child I always had straight teeth, but I loved candy, sweets and all that jazz so of course I had a few cavities. Unfortunately, I also had weaker teeth, so the weak teeth mixed with sugar created holes in my front three teeth. (That's right the ones directly in the front, lol). Over time those holes began to get bigger, more noticeable and later started to chip. I started the process of getting them fixed towards the end of eighth grade, but it was a long and expensive process. I'm sure that you can imagine the horror of starting high school dark-skinned with messed up teeth and not having any of my friends, except my sister. Yay! The cycle continued.

Literally, for almost the first whole year of high school, I followed my sister around every morning. One, because I didn't know anyone yet and two, I didn't want to make myself noticeable and become the prey of my next bully. That didn't work. The bully still found me my ninth-grade year. I never had any other encounters with her except when she decided to whittle me down. She would talk about and pick on any and everything she could find from my clothes to my weight. Since I was older, I knew that hurt people hurt people but that still never made it hurt less.

So, bullies, skin tone, teeth and all that I was dealing with and now on top of all of that I had the fear of being rejected. It's interesting the things that don't bother you when you are younger and yet they become cataclysmic when you get older. Long story short, I would visit and spend time, a little here and there, with my father over the years but nothing big or mandatory. When I was younger it didn't bother me because of course I'm young, I was loved and loving my fun little life but the older I got the bigger the hole in my heart grew from something missing (of course Jesus filled that hole but let's not skip ahead).

The older I became the more my feelings about my absentee father began to evolve. I didn't understand what was so wrong with me that my own father didn't want me or so I thought. That unhealthy thought life created the fear in me of being rejected. So for most males, even if they were walking past me, I had an automatic guard up for the fear of being picked on because them picking on me was the same as them rejecting me and that was my ultimate fear.

If you haven't caught on, one cycle precedes another. And my negative cycles were not excluded.

After my cycle of fearing rejection, came my cycle of anger. It was as if anger was waiting for me at the door (lol). And I was VERY angry. I was angry because I had to go through that because of my father and his failure to fight to do better… or fight for me. Now, looking back, I realize this was a misplaced responsibility. But just imagine what it felt like to be trying to build up my confidence being a dark skinned girl, with messed up teeth, that was afraid of always being the target and rejected and now this. Daddy issues.

But thanks be to God that He healed all of this and then some. It was a long, long, long and difficult journey at times but now I know that if I didn't go through those; I would never have embraced the truth that God created me in His perfect image! All these hurts needed to happen in my past, for me to have my now (and I love my now). I know that chocolate is in! All variations and colors. All beautiful works of art were created by my father THE king who doesn't make mistakes.

I now know that I needed that feeling of fear and rejection to keep my focus on him (God). I also now have a good relationship with my Father. When we give others the grace that we also desperately need, we are able to build meaningful relationships, no matter the history.

And even though I still have one more step for my teeth I did end up getting a flipper for my front teeth so now they're all there unless I take them out. But even in this season of waiting, I have peace. Those who are for me and love me, will do so no matter what I look like. Those who are not, don't have any say over my future. It's all good!

TAKEAWAY LESSON

Mechelle learned that people will project their own insecurities onto you, but it is up to you to decide how you will respond. Will you fold or will you blossom? Consider the most beautiful flowers… they are usually fed through compost or manure. The things that you wouldn't think have any benefit are repurposed to *give life*. What you go through is meant to grow you. You just have to push… and you have to be diligent about protecting your seedlings.

Don't allow anything to cause you to give ground to the enemy. Your anger, your hurt, your disappointment… use it all as fuel to pursue God harder. Push for relationship with Him so that He can begin to share with you His purpose and plan for your life. He doesn't want you to feel abandoned on the battlefield. He wants to equip you. The fiery darts are not always going to look like arrows, but they will pierce you, nonetheless. The enemy wants to distract us from the truth that we are created in the image of God and therefore not a mistake. If we lose sight of our worth, the enemy can cause us to put down your shield during an attack. You can't afford to do that, my love. Change your mentality about what warfare really is and you will begin to properly use the weapons of the spirit.

AFFIRMATIONS

I was created in His image. I am beautiful.

The devil wars against me not because I am weak, but because I am strong.

I have been created for and with purpose.

My value to God is not based on my ability or attributes. It is based on His intentional creation of me.

SCRIPTURE BANK

Psalm 9:1 *I will praise thee, O Lord, with my whole heart; I will shew forth all thy marvelous works. (KJV)*

Psalm 42:9-11 *9 I will say to God, my rock, "Why have you forgotten me? Why must I go about in sorrow because of the enemy's oppression?" 10 My adversaries taunt me, as if crushing my bones, while all day long they say to me, "Where is your God?" 11 Why, my soul, are you so dejected?*

Why are you in such turmoil? Put your hope in God, for I will still praise him, my Savior and my God. (CSB)

Ephesians 6:11-13 **11** *Put on the whole armor of God, that ye may be able to stand against the wiles of the devil.* **12** *For we wrestle not against flesh and blood, but against principalities, against powers, against the rulers of the darkness of this world, against spiritual wickedness in high places.* **13** *Wherefore take unto you the whole armor of God, that ye may be able to withstand in the evil day, and having done all, to stand.* (KJV)

Genesis 50:20 *You intended to harm me, but God intended it for good to accomplish what is now being done, the saving of many lives.* (NIV)

Matthew 16:19 *I will give you the keys of the kingdom of heaven; whatever you bind on earth will be bound in heaven, and whatever you loose on earth will be loosed in heaven.* (NIV)

PRAYER OF FORGIVENESS

Father God, in the name of Jesus. We come to you to say thank you for another opportunity to forgive and be forgiven. We understand that hurt people hurt people, but the cycle stops with us. Thank you for opening our hearts to your love and our minds to your Word. We no longer carry the past hurts, disappointments and fears that fed our unforgiveness. We lay those things at your feet. In their place, we pick up the banner of love and we carry it before us as we wage war against the enemy and his fiery darts. We will not be bound by anything but your love and grace. Love rules here. We thank you for this gift of renewal. In Jesus' name, amen.

We will not be bound by anything but your love and grace.

Day 2
Love Freely Given

LEAH

When we think that a woman is prettier than we are, we tend to believe that she also has more favor. It's a weird little trick that our mind plays on us. But God doesn't base His love or care for us on how we look. He loves us despite ourselves, our actions and our inability to fully commit to His plan. He looks inside our hearts and loves us anyway. There is no competition that we must win to gain His approval or attention. We just have to love Him with our whole hearts.

I wish that Leah had known that. That she didn't have to spend her life making up for the trickery of her father or not being as beautiful as her sister. I wish that I could just hold her close and share with her the goodness of God and His provision. And that His "provision" is not always what we want it to be, but it is everything that we need it to be. A lack of love from her husband did not diminish the impact of God's love toward her.

Leah is a beautiful reminder that we do not have to force God to love us; we just have to accept His love. He wants to care for us. Even when no one else wants us. Most people focus on the passionate love that Jacob had for Rachel and yet it is Leah who gave birth to Judah, who would one day lead the tribe that Jesus would be born into.

If we become passionate about the things of God, the slights of those around us will matter less. Leah never measured up to Rachel in Jacob's eyes and yet

God determined that Leah was the perfect conduit for the salvation of the world. That's huge. It's not about who doesn't see your worth, it is about the One who called you worthy.

It is so important to realize that the battle is not always with other people. It can be with ourselves. Either with our minds, poor choices or factors we have no control over. None of that changes the outcome of victory. God had already seen to it that the pain in Leah's life would not go unanswered.

Leah gave birth to three sons and each time she hoped that it would cause Jacob to love her. But when she gave birth to Judah, she focused on thanking God for His love… and that was the son who would make history. There is a lesson there. You can't change a person's heart; they have to want to change it. You can't force someone to see you, they have to want to search for you. When she focused less on her problems and more on her blessings, she received peace. Stop worrying about who doesn't love you and start focusing on who does.

God blessed Leah's womb in a way that made it clear she was not forgotten. And He has not forgotten you either. You just have to trust Him.

I encourage you to read Leah's story with fresh eyes. There is beauty in the plain woman who remained steadfast in her love to a man who didn't understand the blessing he had received. By being given both Leah and Rachel, his line would be the foundation for Israel.

Fun Detour:
Go to Genesis 29; 30; 49:31 and Ruth 4:11 for one of the most explosive turnaround stories in the Bible. Hint: *Rachel* ends up being jealous of *Leah*.

AFFIRMATIONS

There is no competition.

I am loved for who I am and not how I look.

I am worth the pursuit.

SCRIPTURE BANK

Habakkuk 3:17-18 *17 Though the fig tree does not bud and there are no grapes on the vines, though the olive crop fails and the fields produce no food, though there are no sheep in the pen and no cattle in the stalls, 18 yet I will rejoice in the Lord, I will be joyful in God my Savior. (NIV)*

Psalm 42:1 *As the deer pants for the water brooks, so pants my soul for You, O God. (NKJV)*

Psalm 42:8 *The Lord will send his faithful love by day; his song will be with me in the night— a prayer to the God of my life. (CSB)*

PRAYER OF ACCEPTANCE

Father God, in the name of Jesus. I am thankful for the unmerited grace and mercy that you have shown to me. For the love that you have freely given to me. You are the greatest to ever do it and I'm in awe that you would take the time out to think of me. Because you don't have to, but you do. Daily. In this moment, I open my heart to your love, and I accept that I am enough. I don't have to fight for your attention. Thank you for reminding me that you are present in every moment, every season, every thought, every heartbreak and every milestone. You're my best friend. Thank you for teaching me how to be loved. In Jesus' name, amen.

I don't have to fight for your attention.

Day 3
Go Anyway

ESTHER

If you have ever listened to one of my podcasts or watched my videos, then you know how much I love the story of Esther. Like LOVE it. If you're new to her story go read the entire book of Esther. We've got time.

Now that you're caught up, I want to focus on Esther 4:1-17. And let's go ahead and put special emphasis on verses 14 through 16. Mordecai had to remind Esther that whether or not she fulfilled her duty, provision would come for God's people. However, she would lose everything that she was trying to protect by sitting on the sidelines. Let me encourage you with this. If you are afraid that you will lose something by pursuing God, you have already lost.

His purpose and His plan supersede basic desires to be comfortable. We must push past our fear of loss and engage our faith. Not only is He pursuing you, He is putting you into position to pursue Him. He wants to know that He matters to you. That you are willing to lay it on the line, just as He has. Esther had to stop thinking about what she would lose and instead had to consider what could be gained.

Every time that I read that chapter, it hits me. Esther had to physically move from her place of comfort, venture into the unknown and trust that He would meet her there. She had to pursue Him even when it didn't make sense. Because let's be honest, she could have been killed by the King and her people could have still been wiped out by Haman. There was never any guarantee that the King would allow her to speak. But just as Mordecai said, *"For if you remain silent at this time, relief and deliverance for the Jews will arise from another place, but you and your father's family will perish. And who knows but that you have come to your royal position for such a time as this?"* (Esther 4:14 NIV) She had NOTHING to lose when she really put it all into perspective. Not even her life. Even if she lived longer than the Jews outside of the palace, destruction would still find her. That's often how it is. We think that what we have now is the best we will ever have. But how can that be true when we have not yet experienced tomorrow?

God's plan is not based on nor does it change because of our emotions or feelings. He's still working the plan because He is coming for *you*. And He won't stop until He gets to you. That may require that He nudge you out of your current position. It may require you to sacrifice your perception of blessings. It may require you to stand in the gap for someone else. It may require you to step forward, use your voice and enhance someone's understanding of who He *really* is. There is a requirement to the act of pursuit. And that requirement is movement.

Just as God pursued Esther's heart, she had to pursue His plan. Mordecai helped to open her eyes that God was coming to raise her up for His glory.

AFFIRMATIONS

I was created for and with purpose.

I cannot fail if I follow His plan.

There is nothing that I have that He cannot replace.

SCRIPTURE BANK

Isaiah 58:11 *The Lord will guide you always; he will satisfy your needs in a sun-scorched land and will strengthen your frame. You will be like a well-watered garden, like a spring whose waters never fail.* (NIV)

Ephesians 1:11-12 ***11** In him we were also chosen, having been predestined according to the plan of him who works out everything in conformity with the purpose of his will, **12** in order that we, who were the first to put our hope in Christ, might be for the praise of his glory.* (NIV)

Matthew 6:31-33 ***31** So do not worry, saying, 'What shall we eat?' or 'What shall we drink?' or 'What shall we wear?' **32** For the pagans run after all these things, and your heavenly Father knows that you need them. **33** But seek first his kingdom and his righteousness, and all these things will be given to you as well.* (NIV)

Psalm 90:17 *May the favor of the Lord our God rest on us; establish the work of our hands for us— yes, establish the work of our hands.* (NIV)

Psalm 112:6-8 ***6** Surely the righteous will never be shaken; they will be remembered forever. **7** They will have no fear of bad news; their hearts are steadfast, trusting in the Lord. **8** Their hearts are secure, they will have no fear; in the end they will look in triumph on their foes.* (NIV)

2 Timothy 1:7 *For the Spirit God gave us does not make us timid, but gives us power, love and self-discipline.* (NIV)

Deuteronomy 31:6 *Be strong and courageous. Do not be afraid or terrified because of them, for the Lord your God goes with you; he will never leave you nor forsake you.* (NIV)

PRAYER OF DISCOMFORT

Father God, in the name of Jesus. Thank you for opening my eyes to the cage that comfort is. I want to pursue you even when I am weary and don't understand the plan. Give me that tenacious spirit to embrace discomfort. Father guide me in your righteousness and protect me from my complacency. Thank you for shifting the atmosphere and turning up the heat. I'm moving. I'm coming. My faith has been activated. Thank you for the nudge. In Jesus' name, amen.

Give me that tenacious spirit to embrace discomfort.

Day 4
Your End = His Beginning

MARY MAGDALENE

There are a lot of stories and rumors that still run rampant about MM. You would think that we are back in high school the way that folks keep the rumor mill going. But I don't plan to focus on the rumors. I want to dive into her truth.

She was at the bottom of the barrel. And I mean that literally. Sis had seven demons attached to her. If you don't believe me, read her story for yourself in Matthew 27:56, 61; 28:1; Mark 15:40, 47; 16:1-19; Luke 8:2; 24:10; John 19:25; 20:1-18.

MM's life is proof that when you think your life is over, it's really your beginning. Oftentimes, it takes hitting rock bottom or a cataclysmic event to get us to stop trying to do everything on our own. We must be completely broken before we give God the opportunity to step in. It's not the best practice, but it's often reality.

After Jesus cast out the seven demons, MM is noted for being one of His most devoted followers. When she was released from her torment she pursued an active connection and relationship with the father. She left what she had for what she could gain. Jesus saw her and pursued her spirit in the enemy's camp. In turn, MM pursued relationship and remained devoted to Him for the rest of her life. In fact, after all the other disciples (outside of John) abandoned Him during the crucifixion… she was there. She was also the first to see Him when He rose from the grave.

That tells me that MM had tapped into the idea that as debased as her life was when controlled by the demons, so too it could be worthwhile attached to Christ. God honored that mentality by showing favor to her, repeatedly. It wasn't about where she came from or had been through. Or even what people may have said about her. It was about her pursuing Him and not looking back.

Let's do a quick recap of the favor shown to MM:

1. She was the first to see the empty grave.
2. She was the first to see Jesus after He rose from the dead.
3. She was the first person Jesus spoke to after He rose from the dead.
4. She was the first person to carry the good news of His resurrection.

MM continued to stretch her capacity to serve and love Christ daily from the moment He healed her. And shouldn't we do the same? We may not have seven demons attached to us, but He has broken soul ties, removed us from toxic situations, provided for us, protected us and given us daily opportunities to bless others. It's time to stretch. It's time to gear up and show up.

AFFIRMATIONS

What had me couldn't keep me.

My position is intentional.

He sees my potential and elevates me to purpose.

SCRIPTURE BANK

Romans 3:23 *For all have sinned and come short of the glory of God. (NKJV)*
Romans 5:8 *But God demonstrates his own love for us in this: While we were still sinners, Christ died for us. (NKJV)*

Romans 8:28 And we know that all things work together for good to those who love God, to those who are the called according to His purpose. (NKJV)

Acts 17:27 *He did this so that they might seek God, and perhaps they might reach out and find him, though he is not far from each one of us. (CSB)*

John 1:12 *Yet to all who did receive him, to those who believed in his name, he gave the right to become children of God. (NIV)*

Galatians 5:25 *Since we live by the Spirit, let us keep in step with the Spirit. (NIV)*

Colossians 2:13-14 **13** *When you were dead in your sins and in the uncircumcision of your flesh, God made you alive with Christ. He forgave us all our sins,* **14** *having canceled the charge of our legal indebtedness, which stood against us and condemned us; he has taken it away, nailing it to the cross. (NIV)*

Psalm 34:17-19 **17** *The righteous cry out, and the Lord hears them; he delivers them from all their troubles.* **18** *The Lord is close to the brokenhearted and saves those who are crushed in spirit.* **19** *The righteous person may have many troubles, but the Lord delivers him from them all. (NIV)*

Romans 12:21 *Do not be overcome by evil but overcome evil with good. (NIV)*

Deuteronomy 28:7 *The Lord will grant that the enemies who rise up against you will be defeated before you. They will come at you from one direction but flee from you in seven. (NIV)*

PRAYER OF LOYALTY

Father God, in the name of Jesus. Thank you for standing with me day in and day out. Thank you for fighting my battles, even if I was the one to shoot the first shot. Thank you for being committed to the purpose you gave and loyal to the woman I am becoming. Lord, continue to give me opportunities to express my love and adoration for you. Continue to begin conversations that will stretch my loyalty to you. Lord, I want it to be clear to everyone who meets me that I am a Jesus Girl. My entire identity is found in you because you eradicated my old one. Help me to focus on what you have called out of me. That I may be that woman. Teach me to be as loyal to my purpose as you were to the cross. In Jesus' name, amen.

Day 5
Go the Distance

JAEL

If you've never heard of Jael, let me introduce you to a true rider. When it came down to it, she didn't hesitate to play her position and get the job *done*. Now is the time to not only know your position, but to play your position.

Today we are going to study Judges 4.

Have you ever been in a situation and you had no idea how God was going to handle it… and He ends up just setting the solution in your lap? I'm talking about that random, confidence boosting, couldn't get any better, had to be God's solution. That's what happened with Jael.

Sisera, a powerful general in Canaan, had been routed by the Israelite army and fled on foot to what he thought was a place of refuge. Little did he know that Jael had seen an opportunity for vindication and was willing to trust God's timing. Lesson? Just because someone in your circle has a relationship with someone, that doesn't mean you should. Be careful about who you attach to. They may not have attached back. Sisera assumed the attachment was mutual for all members of the house of Heber.

Jael was able to reassure Sisera enough for him to lie down in the middle of battle and rest. We must be careful about who we allow to lull us into a false sense of security! Not only did she get him to rest but he was so comfortable that she was able to drive a stake through his head, without issue. God showed her Sisera's weakness and she rallied her strength. I told you that she was a rider!

While the Bible doesn't talk about Jael any other time, I'm hard pressed to believe that this woman did not know the voice or recognize the hand of God. She pursued relationship with Him, even when her husband had moved the family outside of the protection and the will of God. Jael was not only steadfast, but she stood at the ready. Verse 18 says she went out to meet him. That makes me think that she was keeping watch. That's the same way we must be when looking for movement from God. We must be in position, we have to be watchful and we have to be prepared to act with a moment's notice.

Loves, there will be times in our journey of pursuit that we have to stand still and wait for His next move. Don't get so anxious that you get ahead of Him. Search for Him in the everyday and then be patient as He shows you the next step. He may just show up on your doorstep… you just have to be there to open the door.

Jael was there and available and God helped to bring victory for His people through her. I'm sure that when God looked and saw that it was Jael who Sisera would flee to, He didn't worry. In fact, He probably thought "oh, Jael has got this. I'm good." She didn't disappoint.

AFFIRMATIONS

Hesitation will cost me my life.

Timing is everything, especially when ending friendships.

Sometimes "pursuit" means standing still.

SCRIPTURE BANK

John 10:27 *My sheep listen to my voice; I know them, and they follow me. (NIV)*

Proverbs 3:5-6 **5** *Trust in the Lord with all your heart and lean not on your own understanding;* **6** *in all your ways submit to him, and he will make your paths straight. (NIV)*

Isaiah 41:10 *So do not fear, for I am with you; do not be dismayed, for I am your God. I will strengthen you and help you; I will uphold you with my righteous right hand. (NIV)*

Romans 8:31-32 **31** *What, then, shall we say in response to these things? If God is for us, who can be against us?* **32** *He who did not spare his own Son, but gave him up for us all—how will he not also, along with him, graciously give us all things? (NIV)*

1 Peter 5:8-9 **8** *Be alert and of sober mind. Your enemy the devil prowls around like a roaring lion looking for someone to devour.* **9** *Resist him, standing firm in the faith, because you know that the family of believers throughout the world is undergoing the same kind of sufferings. (NIV)*

Romans 8:37 *No, in all these things we are more than conquerors through him who loved us. (NIV)*

1 Corinthians 15:57 *But thanks be to God! He gives us the victory through our Lord Jesus Christ. (NIV)*

2 Thessalonians 3:3 *But the Lord is faithful, and he will strengthen you and protect you from the evil one. (NIV)*

Joshua 23:10 *One of you routs a thousand, because the Lord your God fights for you, just as he promised. (NIV)*

PRAYER OF COURAGE

Father in heaven, you are good. We trust in your plan and your ability to see the future. Thank you for guiding our friendships and identifying the weak links. Help us to be bold in our faith as we wait for direction from you. Keep us within your perfect will and forgive us when we stray into your permissive will. We are bold as lions and we thank you for the courage to do the hard things. The bloody things. The painful things. We will not squirm when asked to share our love for you and we will not back down when adhering to your Word. Thank you for courage. In Jesus' name, amen.

Week Two Exercise

Wash your face and let the water just drip. Let every bit of your mask fall away, but don't rush the process. Experience the process. Now go ahead and tone, then moisturize and relax.

I want you to think about the plan you have been working on for the past several months, maybe even years. Where is God in the plan? Have you been trying to strategize for a battle you are ill-equipped to perform in? You have been wearing a full face of make-up to hide your uncertainty about how the game plan will play out. I want you to stop. Turn over your "life plan" and what you *think* gives you value to the One who created you and gave you *dominion* over the earth. It's time to develop your faith action plan.

Take out your phone and pull up your calendar. Or pull out your paper planner if that's what you use. Go through each day for the upcoming two weeks and write in intentional date time with Jesus. Daily. This is not going to be a time for you to flip through your Bible and read the first verse that pops up. This is going to be time for you to clear your mind, read your Word, listen to His voice and begin to write out the plan that HE gives you. Because He will give you one. He's just been waiting for you to let Him get a word in edgewise.

As He shares, write. When He's quiet, read. And when He shifts, move.

Use the next few pages to write down the new plan. You're going to need to come back from time to time to add to it and to review what He has already told you. Be prepared though, the enemy is not going to like that you have educated yourself on proper battle strategy. Put on your armor and never take it off. The battle is here… but it is also already won.

Ephesians 6:10-18 *__10__ Finally, my brethren, be strong in the Lord, and in the power of his might. __11__ Put on the whole armor of God, that ye may be able to stand against the wiles of the devil. __12__ For we wrestle not against flesh and blood, but against principalities, against powers, against the rulers of the darkness of this world, against spiritual wickedness in high places. __13__ Wherefore take unto you the whole armor of God, that ye may be able to withstand in the evil day, and having done all, to stand. __14__ Stand therefore, having your loins girt about with truth, and having on the breastplate of righteousness; __15__ And your feet shod with the preparation of the gospel of peace; __16__ Above all, taking the shield of faith, wherewith ye shall be able to quench all the fiery darts of the wicked. __17__ And take the helmet of salvation, and the sword of the Spirit, which is the word of God: __18__ Praying always with all prayer and supplication in the Spirit, and watching thereunto with all perseverance and supplication for all saints. (NKJV)*

Week 3

Restorative Faith

It is sometimes difficult to accept that He wants to restore those places we have hidden from Him.

I can't believe that we are already beginning our third week together! Can you?! I pray that our time together has been just as sweet for you as it has for me. I'm excited to dive into one of my favorite weeks - restoration. It is sometimes difficult to accept that He wants to restore those places we have hidden from Him. That He wants us to embrace who we are and who we have been called to be. That requires a reworking of our minds and the bondage mentality we have taken on. Let me explain. We have allowed our past hurts and mistakes to dictate how we communicate with God. Our past has completely changed our perception of what our relationship with Him can be.

Let me assure you. He wants a relationship with you. He wants to remind you of your worth and your purpose. His plan concerning you did not change. He just needs for you to open the door and step out. You cannot hide away any longer and you cannot carry the burden alone. Let Him walk with you. Let Him restore you.

Here are some great memory verses!

John 14:27 *Peace I leave with you; my peace I give you. I do not give to you as the world gives. Do not let your hearts be troubled and do not be afraid.* (NIV)

Romans 8:28 *And we know that in all things God works for the good of those who love Him, who have been called according to his purpose.* (NIV)

Romans 8:38-39 *For I am convinced that neither death nor life, neither angels nor demons, neither the present nor the future, nor any powers, neither height nor depth, nor anything else in creation, will be able to separate us from the love of God that is in Christ Jesus our Lord.* (NIV)

Please note that there will be fewer pictures included in this week, due to the sensitive subject matter and need to protect Destiny's identity.

Day 1
Broken Not Worthless

DESTINY

Let me forewarn you that Destiny's story is one that will make you sad and angry at the same time. You will question the process of God because you will have overlooked the provision of God. But I want you to know that Destiny's story is truly one of redemption and freedom. Even when we are driven into the wilderness, God will be with us keeping an eye on the path and the way home.

As Destiny began to talk a simple prayer rose in my heart.

God help us to see your hand, even when your face is hidden. Remind us that your love has no beginning and no end. Even in our brokenness you have a purpose for us in mind. A purpose that will defy the odds and lead others to you. You are grooming us to be leaders in your army. So, Lord, thank you for covering us even when we feel that we are alone and forgotten. In our darkest hour you are the little lamp that guides our feet. Keep our eyes trained on you instead of shifting to the shadows around us. Your grace is sufficient, and your victory is sure. Thank you for including us in that plan of provision. In Jesus' name, amen.

Now, let's meet Destiny.

I was molested by two people. One male and one female. Both were family members. The female was caught at a family gathering by a cousin who walked in on the act. The female, my cousin, was a year and a half older than

I was. Sadly, no one stepped in to properly handle the situation. That moment was divine and yet it was missed. They just separated us. One of the scariest things is seeing the rescuer and not being rescued. Yet this happens more often than people care to acknowledge. *We have this expectation that those that love us, will rescue us when they see us drowning but in reality they are not spiritually or mentally equipped to wade out into the deep to aid us. It's time to sign up for swimming lessons.*

The male, my brother, sexually abused me until I was 13 years old. At 13 years old it turned into physical abuse. He would lash out and I would try to fight back. Full on knock down and drag out fights. His sexual abuse was never discovered.

One of the most hurtful things he said was, "you don't have to worry about getting raped, because people don't rape fat people". Not only did he not acknowledge what he had *done*, but he created a *narrative* that was not his story to tell.

Rape has nothing to do with the attributes (or lack thereof) of the victim and everything to do with the mentality of the assailant.

In 9th grade, I tried to kill myself by cutting. It didn't work, so I decided to jump in the street in front of a car. No cars came. I was so upset that I couldn't do it. That God wouldn't let me die. My friends found me and told my parents. I tried to talk to my mom about it and she didn't and perhaps couldn't, really listen. She blamed someone else for influencing what she considered to be poor choices.

It's hard to swim against the tide when you have already reached your peak level of exhaustion.

The sad truth is that some parents aren't ready to believe that their children have been hurt while in their care. It's impossible for them to acknowledge what is inevitably perceived as a failure because their love blinds them to their humanity.

But one day my mom finally asked why I was physically fighting my brother. When I finally revealed the sexual abuse, she refused to believe me. Looking back, it's a little unnerving that it took so long for her to ask or even address the turmoil that was evident between he and I. *It's easier to throw someone a life jacket than it is to pull them into the boat.*

From that point on I decided to keep it to myself and once I reached my breaking point, I decided I would kill him if he touched me again. That was at 21 years old. When I reached that point, I realized that I needed to confront him and get to a place of mutual understanding about how hurtful his actions were.

What truly terrified me is that after we would fight, he would ask why we didn't have a better relationship. As if he had no idea what he had done. *You can't keep facing a wave hell bent on taking you under. Invest in a surfboard.*

After I mustered the strength to talk to him, he said that it didn't happen and that I was lying. He was belligerent and angry to the point that he threatened to kill himself. It's scary to hear that your brother is willing to kill himself to prove a point, what's scarier is that a part of me wanted to do it for him and yet…I knew that God didn't want me to be responsible for his death.

2 Chronicles 20:15 *And he said, Hearken ye, all Judah, and ye inhabitants of Jerusalem, and thou king Jehoshaphat, Thus saith the Lord unto you, Be not afraid nor dismayed by reason of this great multitude; for the battle is not yours, but God's. (KJV)*

But instead of embracing that the victory is *won*, I created walls around myself that I thought were meant to protect me but now at 27, I realize that I was really hiding from myself and the beauty that God has given me. I have a purpose. I have worth. I am better than. I am more than. No matter what the situation is, no matter how dark and how unworthy we feel about whatever happened to us, God is always protecting, providing and keeping His children as His own.

There is a hedge of protection around me and yet, those meant for me, have found me and loved me. The darkness won't win. I know for a fact that God loves me simply because He kept me!

TAKEAWAY LESSON

There is never a time that God deserts us, and we cannot thwart His love for us. He sees us in our broken places and takes the time to re-work those pieces into a one of a kind works of art. There is an intentional plan of purpose in place for each of us. Regardless of the action or inaction of others.

We have the authority to call our healing and wholeness forth. We just have to believe in its finality.

AFFIRMATIONS

I am worth the fight.

I am beautifully broken and that is okay.

I'm not on a shelf, I'm on the Potter's wheel.

SCRIPTURE BANK

Joshua 1:9 *Have not I commanded thee? Be strong and of a good courage; be not afraid, neither be thou dismayed: for the LORD thy God is with thee whithersoever thou goest. (KJV)*

Psalm 103:13 *As a father has compassion on his children, so the LORD has compassion on those who fear him. (NIV)*

Psalm 139:14 *I will praise thee; for I am fearfully and wonderfully made: marvelous are thy works; and that my soul knoweth right well. (KJV)*

Deuteronomy 1:29-31 **29** *Then I said unto you, dread not, neither be afraid of them.* **30** *The Lord your God which goeth before you, he shall fight for you, according to all that he did for you in Egypt before your eyes;* **31** *And in the wilderness, where thou hast seen how that the Lord thy God bare thee, as a man doth bear his son, in all the way that ye went, until ye came into this place. (KJV)*

Exodus 14:13 *And Moses said unto the people, Fear ye not, stand still, and see the salvation of the Lord, which he will shew to you today: for the Egyptians whom ye have seen today, ye shall see them again no more forever. (KJV)*

1 Corinthians 16:13 *Watch ye, stand fast in the faith, quit you like men, be strong. (KJV)*

PRAYER OF WHOLENESS

Father God, I love you. Even when I don't understand, you remain. And so I thank you for the opportunity to love you a little harder from my broken places. Thank you for being the kind of father who comes to find me where I am. There is no hurt that you have not felt, no anger you have not held and no tears you have not dried. You are good in all ways, always. Thank you for reminding me that I am whole because you fill the empty places. I am enough because you have declared it to the heavens. Thank you for contentment as I navigate the storm of self-actualization. In Jesus' name, amen.

Day 2
Unlikely Protection

RAHAB

Have you ever been in a situation and you had no idea how God was going to work it out, but He did? And He did it in the most surprising way? That's the story of Rahab.

Rahab's story is in Joshua 2:1-24 and trust me this is a story that you won't be able to walk away from. Let's just say that Rahab was a successful businesswoman, who happened to work in the prostitution industry.

She was also a woman who knew a winning team when she saw one and she didn't mind betting on the odds. Rahab hid the two spies that Joshua had sent into Jericho because she feared their God and knew that this might be her only chance of surviving what was to come. So not only did she provide the spies with unlikely protection but it is unlikely that she would have received protection or been spared had she not turned her back on her own people. Lesson? You won't always know where your help is coming from, you just have to be in the correct position to receive it.

Not only is God in constant pursuit of your heart but He has sent protection to cover you wherever you go. Wherever. You. Go. It doesn't matter if you are running from Him or not, He's not going to leave you unprotected, you just have to be aware enough to recognize His hand when He reaches out to you. Rahab saw the hand of God and helped to save her entire family from destruction. God wasn't worried about her being a prostitute, He was interested to see if she would provide care for His children and turn from the ways of her people and serve Him with abandon. She did it without hesitation.

I have found that in my pursuit, there is not such a great distance that I must travel. I just have to make a conscious effort to look for His hand and then grab hold. He will honor that. Just as He honored Rahab by including her in the ancestry of Jesus. There isn't a higher honor.

Don't worry about the mistakes you have made in your past. Focus on making the conscious choice to choose Him today. Choose restoration.

AFFIRMATIONS

I have the power to lead my entire family to Christ.

I have the honor of being included among God's children.

God trusts me to trust Him.

SCRIPTURE BANK

Psalm 121:1-8 *I will lift up mine eyes unto the hills, from whence cometh my help. 2 My help cometh from the Lord, which made heaven and earth. 3 He will not suffer thy foot to be moved: he that keepeth thee will not slumber. 4 Behold, he that keepeth Israel shall neither slumber nor sleep. 5 The Lord is thy keeper: the Lord is thy shade upon thy right hand. 6 The sun shall not smite thee by day, nor the moon by night. 7 The Lord shall preserve thee from all evil: he shall preserve thy soul. 8 The Lord shall preserve thy going out and thy coming in from this time forth, and even for evermore.* (KJV)

Psalm 23:1-6 *The Lord is my shepherd; I shall not want. 2 He maketh me to lie down in green pastures: he leadeth me beside the still waters. 3 He restoreth my soul: he leadeth me in the paths of righteousness for his name's sake.* **4** *Yea, though I walk through the valley of the shadow of death, I will fear no evil: for thou art with me; thy rod and thy staff they comfort me.* **5** *Thou preparest a table before me in the presence of mine enemies: thou anointest my head with oil; my cup runneth over.* **6** *Surely goodness and mercy shall follow me all the days of my life: and I will dwell in the house of the Lord forever. (KJV)*

Matthew 6:33 *But seek ye first the kingdom of God, and his righteousness; and all these things shall be added unto you. (KJV)*

PRAYER OF WISDOM

Father God in the name of Jesus. Thank you for your wisdom. Thank you for showing me how to put your wisdom to good use and to see your hand moving. Lord, thank you for the opportunities and open doors you have placed before me. Help me to know which ones are for me and which ones are not. Thank you for consistently making a way out of no way and giving me a platform to applaud your goodness. I thank you right now for preparing me to save my people. It won't be done by force but by your spirit and through your wisdom. In Jesus' name, amen.

Day 3
Covered

TAMAR

I want you to join me in the book of 2 Samuel chapter 13. Read it carefully. Take note of the following:

1. If you don't control your flesh, your flesh will control you.
2. Sin will blind you to its true intent, until it has sufficiently trapped you.
3. If your "friend" encourages you to sin, they are aiding in your spiritual annihilation. They're not your friend.
4. Just because someone of influence asks you to do something, that doesn't automatically warrant a "yes".
5. Not properly addressing an offense, even one caused by a family member, will cause your dissatisfaction to fester and pollute your mind.
6. Just because you have access to something, that doesn't mean that it belongs to you.

Tamar was the daughter of King David, the sister of Absalom and the half-sister of Amnon. She was also a virgin and incredibly beautiful. You would think that she had no worries or cares. However, let me point out to you that we never truly know someone else's battles. Seen or unseen. She had no idea that Amnon coveted her or that he would be willing to sacrifice everything to have her. Amnon's battle with lust would be his undoing and a gateway for the enemy to directly attack the household of David.

And yet, it didn't have to be that way. In fact, when Tamar realized that Amnon intended to rape her she *offered herself* to him but pleaded that he do it the right way. All he had to do was ask the King for her. Yet he refused. How often has God clearly shown us an alternative but instead we choose the option we know is wrong? I'd dare say too many times to count. Tamar was not withholding herself from Amnon but was instead trying to cover his disgrace and her impending humiliation by reminding him of order. Isn't that just like our father? He withholds nothing from us but only asks that we be obedient and follow His will. Simple.

There was such a spirit of wisdom in Tamar, even in her distress. She knew that once she left Amnon's chambers that a series of events would occur that could not be undone. This man had hurt and disgraced her beyond compare and yet she was willing to remain in his home and be considered his. If only to lessen the shame he had created. Again, Amnon refused to heed her warning and sent her away. He had her thrown out which is incredible considering *he* raped *her*.

Absalom provided a haven for Tamar. Technically because of the disgrace of losing her virginity she was unclean and unwanted. However, even though she was no longer considered "pure", God ensured that her honor was covered, and her dignity restored. It took two years but Amnon paid with his life for the life he denied to Tamar.

Now let me be clear, I don't think that God wanted Absalom to kill Amnon, but David failed to properly and fully address the sin of Amnon. It is no wonder that sin began to permeate the house and hatred ate at the heart of Absalom. If David had addressed the behavior of Amnon when he was pining away over Tamar or, in the alternative, punished him after his heinous act, the story might have ended differently. The lesson is this, we will leave the perfect will of God because of our emotions and begin to operate in His permissive will and create more of a mess than the one we were trying to clean up. It is imperative that we immediately acknowledge and call sin what it is, SIN.

And let me give you this for free; watch out for people like Jonadab. He encouraged Amnon to rape Tamar and he knew of Absalom's plan to kill Amnon in retaliation. People who are always aware of the gossip are typically at the root of it.

AFFIRMATIONS

God will always provide a safe place for me.

No one can take away my identity in Christ.

God will restore my honor.

SCRIPTURE BANK

Psalm 71:20-21 **20** *Thou, which hast shewed me great and sore troubles, shalt quicken me again, and shalt bring me up again from the depths of the earth.* **21** *Thou shalt increase my greatness, and comfort me on every side.* (KJV)

Isaiah 61:7 *For your shame ye shall have double; and for confusion they shall rejoice in their portion: therefore in their land they shall possess the double: everlasting joy shall be unto them.* (KJV)

Jeremiah 30:17 *For I will restore health unto thee, and I will heal thee of thy wounds, saith the Lord; because they called thee an Outcast, saying, This is Zion, whom no man seeketh after.* (KJV)

1 John 5:4 *For whatsoever is born of God overcometh the world: and this is the victory that overcometh the world, even our faith.* (KJV)

1 Peter 5:10 *But the God of all grace, who hath called us unto his eternal glory by Christ Jesus, after that ye have suffered a while, make you perfect, stablish, strengthen, settle you.* (KJV)

John 14:1 *Let not your heart be troubled: ye believe in God, believe also in me. (KJV)*

Ephesians 4:29 *Let no corrupt communication proceed out of your mouth, but that which is good to the use of edifying, that it may minister grace unto the hearers. (KJV)*

Leviticus 19:16 *Thou shalt not go up and down as a talebearer among thy people: neither shalt thou stand against the blood of thy neighbour; I am the Lord. (KJV)*

Proverbs 10:18 *He that hideth hatred with lying lips, and he that uttereth a slander, is a fool. (KJV)*

Proverbs 11:13 *A talebearer revealeth secrets: but he that is of a faithful spirit concealeth the matter. (kJV)*

Proverbs 16:28 *A froward man soweth strife: and a whisperer separateth chief friends. (KJV)*

Romans 1:28-32 **28** *And even as they did not like to retain God in their knowledge, God gave them over to a reprobate mind, to do those things which are not convenient;* **29** *Being filled with all unrighteousness, fornication, wickedness, covetousness, maliciousness; full of envy, murder, debate, deceit, malignity; whisperers,* **30** *Backbiters, haters of God, despiteful, proud, boasters, inventors of evil things, disobedient to parents,* **31** *Without understanding, covenant breakers, without natural affection, implacable, unmerciful:* **32** *Who knowing the judgment of God, that they which commit such things are worthy of death, not only do the same, but have pleasure in them that do them. (KJV)*

PRAYER OF HONOR

Dear Father, thank you for the sweet reminder that our honor is found in you. Your son willingly went to the cross to rectify our disgrace and restore our honor, as your children. You intentionally chose us. We are nothing without you and we seek to be filled with your spirit so that the *earth* shall see your glory. Thank you for pulling us away from the place of self-righteousness and into the embrace of humility. Thank you for providing shelter when we have been thrown out of our place of comfort. Thank you for restoring us back to a place of needing you and your love. There is no comparison to your goodness. Thank you for making the dry places grow. In Jesus' name, amen.

Day 4
There is Still Time

JOCHEBED

I wouldn't be surprised if you didn't recognize her name. She doesn't have a huge role in the Bible, but she has a powerful testimony. She was willing to give up what was rightfully hers to effectuate the will of God. Jochebed is the mother of Moses.

But before I can tell you her story, I must tell you her people's history.

After Joseph and his kin died, a new pharaoh rose to power who had no relationship with Joseph or the Israelites and he became uncomfortable with what he didn't understand and couldn't control. (Exodus 1:8-11) And he made the decision to not only oppress the people of God but to kill their sons because they were a plentiful nation and he feared an uprising. But God had other plans and positioned midwives who would not do Pharaoh's bidding for they feared God. I hope that serves as confirmation that God will strategically place people around you and in your path who will protect and promote the vision that God has for you.

Now to be fair, I think we are all guilty of becoming agitated by people and situations that we cannot understand or control. We like for things to stay within self-made parameters that we ourselves can't quite fit. But we can't kill them, and we cannot kill their children. But let's take that further, you can't kill their dreams, purpose, gifting or ministry. Learn to not only stay in your lane but applaud the person in the lane next to you.

But back to Jochebed, she knew that the Hebrew boys were being killed but when her son was born, she immediately loved him and couldn't part with him. And let's be clear, no mother should have to contemplate giving her child up to die. So, she hid him for three months. And when she could no longer keep him a secret, she put him in a basket in the Nile river. She put her trust in the plan of God even though she had no way of knowing the outcome.

What is special is that her daughter Miriam kept watch over Moses from a distance. Miriam's watch reminds me so much of when the Holy Spirit is watching over us and interceding on our behalf so that we can stay on course. It's also interesting how God quietly slips her into position so that she could not only watch but be ready to respond to when the time came.

Go ahead and read Exodus 2:1-10 to witness the divine appointment of God for baby Moses and Pharaoh's daughter.

Pharaoh's daughter had no reason to care about the well-being of Moses and yet she felt sorry for him. So much so that she did not hesitate to save his life by claiming him for her own. If you are in a place where it seems that God has completely abandoned you to the river and its pull, just know that He may be divinely orchestrating your position of power, prestige and unmerited favor. Moses went from being a slave to a prince in a matter of moments. And while God changed Moses' position, He addressed the needs of Jochebed by restoring her son's life and providing for her financial stability to care for him, as his nurse. God is intentional in His care and His plan.

Even though Jochebed had to give her son up, God gave him back. We must commit to following through and doing everything that He requires of us. Even when it looks like a loss. You will never lose anything by trusting God and following His promptings. She not only saved her son's life, she sustained it.

Give God time to show you who He is and why He's called Jehovah Jireh. The god who provides.

AFFIRMATIONS

You are preparing me for greater than my current circumstance.

I have lost nothing by trusting you.

You will provide not only for me but those connected to me.

SCRIPTURE BANK

Isaiah 46:10 *Declaring the end from the beginning, and from ancient times the things that are not yet done, saying, My counsel shall stand, and I will do all my pleasure. (KJV)*

Revelation 22:13 *I am Alpha and Omega, the beginning and the end, the first and the last. (KJV)*

Isaiah 41:4 *Who has done this and carried it through, calling forth the generations from the beginning? I, the Lord—with the first of them and with the last—I am he. (NIV)*

Proverbs 22:29 *Seest thou a man diligent in his business? He shall stand before kings; he shall not stand before mean men. (KJV)*

PRAYER OF OBEDIENCE

Father God, in the name of Jesus. Thank you for the spirit of obedience. Even when we don't understand, we must act on your Word. Thank you for the desire to push past our own understanding and to rest in your infinite knowledge. You will never ask us to give something up that will leave us in a place of destitution. Whatever we lose will never amount to what we will gain. Thank you for the blessings that you are orchestrating on our behalf. The ones that make absolutely no sense but are exactly what we need. Obedience activates the next level of faith. Thank you for propelling us forward. In Jesus' name, amen.

Day 5
Stick to the Plan

HAGAR

If you remember, I briefly mentioned Hagar last week, in Sarah's story. If you haven't read Genesis 16:1-15; 17:18-20; 21:8-20 and 25:12-18, go ahead and do that now. I'll wait right here for you.

Okay, so now that you're caught up let's dig into a few overlooked truths about Hagar.

1. She didn't pursue favor from Abraham, Sarah gave her to Abraham. So, we can put to rest that she was hot to trot after a married man.
2. Hagar became haughty when she did what her mistress, Sarah, failed to do and she immediately was reminded that she was "out of alignment" with God's initial plan when Abraham had no problem turning her over to Sarah to be abused.
3. Her son became the father of twelve nations, so there was a great lineage that came through her, just as it did Sarah. Remember that your blessing is not diminished by someone else's blessing or someone else's interference.
4. God can do whatever He wants with whomever He wants. He heard Hagar's cry and He promised her that her offspring would be too great to count.

One of the first things that stands out to me in Hagar's story is her lack of choice until she runs away. She's a slave and she has been passed around with no regard to her desires or autonomy. She was a possession. And yet when she became pregnant her demeanor changed. She realized that she had *worth*. Abram had no other children before hers. It's interesting to me that Hagar became prideful in her season of self-awareness. She, quite frankly, forgot that she was still a lowly slave being used as an incubator.

How many of us have forgotten our actual circumstances and begun to operate in our purpose and promise? That's what Hagar did. While her haughtiness is a warning to us not to look down on another's affliction, her mindset shift to embracing that there was more for her than what she saw is vital. We must begin to operate as though the promise has already manifested. We must function with the mentality that any moment the tide can change. You must stick to the plan until the plan is complete.

Hagar tried to run away when it got tough, but the Lord sent her back with the reminder that all things work together for the good and that He had already provided an inheritance for the child she carried. I love that. Even when we fall out of alignment, He is careful to bring us back on course and to propel His plan forward. He could have done this with anyone, but He gave her the honor of a long line of descendants. It wasn't about how out of order Abram and Sarai were. It was about the glory that God could bring about from the situation and Hagar's submission to Him.

It's not about what it looks like or feels like, it's about what He decides. He can do anything with anyone and that includes you. You just have to remember to stick to His plan and don't run when the going gets tough.

The birth of nations is dependent upon your obedience.

AFFIRMATIONS

My past mistakes don't determine God's love for me.

God can use anyone to change the world. It could be me.

I will not forget from where He has brought me, and I will not look down on others in their time of distress.

SCRIPTURE BANK

Romans 8:28 *And we know that all things work together for good to them that love God, to them who are the called according to his purpose. (KJV)*

Proverbs 13:22 *A good man leaveth an inheritance to his children's children: and the wealth of the sinner is laid up for the just. (KJV)*

Ecclesiastes 11:10 *Therefore remove sorrow from thy heart and put away evil from thy flesh: for childhood and youth are vanity. (KJV)*

Joel 2:12 *Therefore also now, saith the Lord, turn ye even to me with all your heart, and with fasting, and with weeping, and with mourning. (KJV)*

Joel 2:13 *And rend your heart, and not your garments, and turn unto the Lord your God: for he is gracious and merciful, slow to anger, and of great kindness, and repenteth him of the evil. (KJV)*

Psalm 13:5-6 *But I have trusted in thy mercy; my heart shall rejoice in thy salvation. I will sing unto the Lord, because he hath dealt bountifully with me. (KJV)*

1 Samuel 16:7 *But the Lord said unto Samuel, Look not on his countenance, or on the height of his stature; because I have refused him: for the Lord seeth not as man seeth; for man looketh on the outward appearance, but the Lord looketh on the heart. (KJV)*

PRAYER OF SUBMISSION

Father God, in the name of Jesus. We thank you for the comfort in submission. We understand that your plans are always better than our own. Thank you for helping us to lay down our egos and focus on growing our humility. We don't have to fight one battle; you have already gone before us and laid waste to our enemies. More importantly, you have stored up wealth for us from our enemy's table. Thank you for being intentional about our care. In Jesus' name, amen.

Week Three Exercise

What is it that you have not trusted Him to heal or restore? What have you not forgiven God for? Be honest. This is between you and Him. I'm asking you to dig deep and answer these tough questions because they have created a stronghold over your faith and it is time that you take back your authority.

You take the authority back by pursuing the truth. And I'm not talking about the superficial "truth" that we see on Instagram, I'm talking about the truth that is His *innate nature*.

Galatians 5:7 *You ran well. Who hindered you from obeying the truth? (NKJV)*

To begin your journey back to the truth, let me supply you with a pair of running shoes, socks, a track suit, a headband, water bottle and mp3 player.

Running shoes: You will likely spend the most money on your shoes because they will need to withstand the most impact. Your running shoes must have enough give to allow your feet to expand, flexibility to bend as the path changes and firmness not to fall apart when the terrain gets rough. He's mapped out the course, you just have to have the shoes that can adapt.

Psalm 119:32 *I will run the way of thy commandments, when thou shalt enlarge my heart. (KJV)*

Socks: If you run for any significant distance without socks, your feet will blister, and your shoes will smell. You can't half lace up. Finish the course and do it to the best of your availability. Someone is cheering for you, but more importantly, someone is waiting to take the baton. Don't let a blister slow you down.

2 Timothy 4:7 *I have fought a good fight, I have finished my course, I have kept the faith. (KJV)*

Track Suit: What you wear on your body is just as important as what you wear on your feet. You need to have clothes that are close to your skin so that there is nothing to pull you backwards. You are going to have to battle against the elements and you need gear that washes easily, breathes well and firmly holds your muscles. You need performance gear that will not only look good but help minimize any distractions.

Romans 5:3-4 *3 And not only so, but we glory in tribulations also: knowing that tribulation worketh patience; 4 And patience, experience; and experience, hope. (KJV)*

Headband: I don't know about you, but I don't plan to sweat my hair out. Period. Don't get off track by having to stop and redo your ponytail. There is a crown waiting for you to replace the headband and keep that hair looking RIGHT.

James 1:12 *Blessed is the man that endureth temptation: for when he is tried, he shall receive the crown of life, which the Lord hath promised to them that love him. (KJV)*

Water bottle: Sis, you don't have time to be dehydrated and you certainly don't have time to break out from drinking a bunch of soda. Begin to quench your thirst with His spirit. His well will never run dry. You just have to be proactive and bring your bottle to fill up.

Psalm 42:1-2 *As the hart panteth after the water brooks, so panteth my soul after thee, O God. 2 My soul thirsteth for God, for the living God: when shall I come and appear before God? (KJV)*

Mp3 player: The only thing that you should be listening to is the Word of God and those who share it. We can't get distracted by the popular music or the dope beat. We must plug into the NPR of heaven.

Hebrews 12:1 *Wherefore seeing we also are compassed about with so great a cloud of witnesses, let us lay aside every weight, and the sin which doth so easily beset us, and let us run with patience the race that is set before us. (KJV)*

Every day this week prepare for your spiritual run by reading these scriptures and then do some form of physical exercise. It can be high or low impact. That's totally up to you. It is just as important to physically train your body as it is to train your mind and feed your spirit. This is not a process that will be mastered overnight, but it will be one that builds your relationship with God in a sweet and intentional way. You are going to have to put in some work to win the prize of regaining the authority over your mind and embracing the truth that God has given all along.

1 Corinthians 9:24-27 *24 Know ye not that they which run in a race run all, but one receiveth the prize? So run, that ye may obtain. 25 And every man that striveth for the mastery is temperate in all things. Now they do it to obtain a corruptible crown; but we an incorruptible. 26 I therefore so run, not as uncertainly; so fight I, not as one that beateth the air: 27 But I keep under my body, and bring it into subjection: lest that by any means, when I have preached to others, I myself should be a castaway. (KJV)*

It's time to release the anger towards God and forgive ourselves. We have a race to run… and a race to win. We can't win without Him.

*We have a race to run …
and a race to win.*

Week 4

Courageous Faith

I can do it. And so can you.

This is it. Our last week together. Yet, I'm not sad. I feel as though I have gained so much strength during this journey of pursuing Him… and identifying my #faithgoals. There are so many truths that I learned as I wrote this book. Truths that I didn't know I needed to take in to gain strength and courage. Y'all, I thought I was strong until I began to read these stories, study these scriptures and pray these prayers. You couldn't tell me that I didn't have any courage before beginning this process.

But you know what? I'm not as sure now that I knew what courage was. Certainly not in the way I know now. Not until I stripped my soul bare and laid out before Him. When I took off my makeup and pretty clothes… I saw myself. And He saw me. And He told me that I can do it. Despite what I have held hidden in my heart for fear of being laughed at or failing. I can do it. And so can you.

It is time that we pick up our courage and we pursue Him with everything that we have. Even when it is uncomfortable and messy. We have to do it anyway. Fear will not hold us captive another moment. Not one more moment.

This last set of memory verses are ones that I hope you will speak into the night when your courage fails and will shout at daybreak when the victory is won.

1 Corinthians 16:13 *Watch ye, stand fast in the faith, quit you like men, be strong. (KJV)*

Deuteronomy 31:6 *Be strong and of a good courage, fear not, nor be afraid of them: for the Lord thy God, he it is that doth go with thee; he will not fail thee, nor forsake thee. (KJV)*

1 Chronicles 28:20 *And David said to Solomon his son, Be strong and of good courage, and do it: fear not, nor be dismayed: for the Lord God, even my God,*

will be with thee; he will not fail thee, nor forsake thee, until thou hast finished all the work for the service of the house of the Lord. (KJV)

Please note that there will be fewer pictures included in this week, due to the sensitive subject matter and need to protect Tammy's identity.

Day 1
Peace Be Still

TAMMY

I remember chatting with Tammy on the phone and as soon as she began her story, my heart squeezed. This is a story not just for married women, but women interested in marriage. Women who must hear the truth about trust and rebuilding it.

I am passionate about marriage and changing the negative narrative. However, to do that I also have to share the tough stories which lead to triumphant victories.

Here's Tammy.

My world turned upside down in 2015. It was then that my husband shared with me that he had a ten-year-old daughter. As you can imagine, this was a complete shock and came out of left field.

I remember that day like it was yesterday.

What really stands out in my memory, is that leading up to the conversation my husband kept telling me that he wanted to pray. I just remember that he paced back and forth before he could get it out.

When he told me, I didn't get upset, curse or fall apart. Ironically, I had been led to pray for multiple days beforehand and right before "the talk". Looking back, I think that was the Holy Spirit preparing me. There was such a sense of peace. He showed me his daughter's picture and I immediately knew that she was his. She looks exactly like our children. In that moment, I believed that I was fully capable of forgiving him. Immediately. But that just meant that I didn't really address the emotions that were bombarding me. I suppressed them. To be honest, I thought that I forgave him, but I don't think that I did because 2016 was a full battle.

And when I say battle, I mean *battle*. When we were at home, we began to argue and fight in a way that we never had. The same way that my heart was numb when he told me, it became fiery. It hit me that he had lived a completely different life for ten years. Completely different. However, with all the uproar in our home there was no one that knew but us and a few family members. It seemed like I had a regular life to everyone else.

But there was a blessing amid that hurt. Had I learned when this had all originally come about, things may have happened differently. Who am I kidding? Things would have been different. We wouldn't be married. Thankfully, I was more spiritually developed in 2015. This made it easier to digest when he told me. Things could have ended horribly if I hadn't been as spiritually mature.

But 2016 still rocked me to my core. Let's just be honest. Even when you know that the end will work out, it doesn't always make the process easier. Even when you forgive someone that doesn't mean you immediately fall back in love. So, one night, I wrestled all night long with the conviction to leave my marriage. I prayed and went through scriptures to validate my feelings and my emotions began to run over. It was the moment of reckoning. In my mind I was done and planned to tell him the next day that I wanted a divorce. However, the next morning I heard the Holy Spirit say "if you love me, the way you say that you love me and to the degree that you say it…you will stay".

Deuteronomy 6:3 *Hear, Israel, and be careful to obey so that it may go well with you and that you may increase greatly in a land flowing with milk and honey, just as the Lord, the God of your ancestors, promised you.*

The Holy Spirit got me out of the bed and I found myself telling my husband that I loved him and I was going to stay and we would work it out. We embraced and I then went and hung his clothes back up in the closet. Where they belonged. And once again, I had that initial peace but as I went through the day I was overcome with emotion and cried. That was the enemy trying to break me down, but I reminded myself of the power of prayer. I began to pray for clarification. I realized that even though I had forgiven my husband I had not forgiven "her".

My husband and I had already gone through the process of counseling, working through our issues and rebuilding our relationship. I had also verbally stated that I forgave her but never actually spoke to her. But I felt the Holy Spirit moving me to call her and forgive her. So, one day I called, and I was completely open about my feelings of hatred, hurt and anger and the desire to forgive her. Once I forgave her, I felt a sense of peace. Which is something that I noticed was happening every time that I followed what God said.

Sisters, there will always be peace when we follow Him.

Of course, the enemy would try to bring back my depression or anger, but the Holy Spirit reminded me to not look back because it was killing me.

That is the biggest lesson that I learned. If you keep looking back, you are going to die. You will completely lose yourself in the past. The devil wants to remind you of "what was" instead of what God intends for you. And trust me, there is nothing better than what He has set aside for you.

If you're wondering, I immediately accepted the child because it is not her fault and I have grown to be cordial to her mother. Now when the enemy tries to bring anything negative back up to me, it rolls off my back. 2016 may have been the year of broken trust and resentment but now I am stronger having faced this battle head on.

I am so thankful that God was there the entire time. That has been the biggest comfort in this entire season of growth. I am also thankful that He did not allow me to find out in the beginning but instead covered me until the right time where I could handle it. I may have been a mental, spiritual and physical mess but I was still able to get up and LIVE.

I believe that He gave me the strength to overcome so that I can remind others that what was will NEVER be better than what is coming. My marriage is stronger than it has ever been, and my mindset is never going to be the same.

Ladies, I encourage you to talk to your husbands. Get to know them daily. There should never be secrets between you of such magnitude. Be the partner that you desire for yourself. Build your husband up and show him how to love you correctly. Your marriage is blessed, but you must constantly anoint it.

Note: This story is *not* meant to tell you how to respond to infidelity. It is an example of one woman's choice to stay and her faith to rebuild her marriage from the ground up. Always seek godly counsel and trust the Holy Spirit when making *your* decision.

TAKEAWAY LESSON

If we want God to heal our brokenness, we must give our brokenness to Him. We can't hold onto it or try to fix it for ourselves. We must let Him have every broken piece. When we face such brutal hurts, we tend to want to roll into a ball and shut out the world, or in the alternative, lash out. Neither is conducive to learning the lesson in the process. We must have a relationship with God for ourselves so that we can begin to identify His voice when He speaks to us. You don't want to get so caught up in your emotions that you miss Him and what He is trying to teach you. No matter the lesson.

AFFIRMATIONS

There is nothing that He can't heal.

Hurt does not define my joy.

There will be peace in the storm.

SCRIPTURE BANK

1 John 4:18 *There is no fear in love; but perfect love casteth out fear: because fear hath torment. He that feareth is not made perfect in love.* (KJV)

Matthew 18:15 *Moreover if thy brother shall trespass against thee, go and tell him his fault between thee and him alone: if he shall hear thee, thou hast gained thy brother.* (KJV)

Colossians 1:20-22 **20** *And, having made peace through the blood of his cross, by him to reconcile all things unto himself; by him, I say, whether they be things in earth, or things in heaven.* **21** *And you, that were sometimes alienated and enemies in your mind by wicked works, yet now hath he reconciled* **22** *In the body of his flesh through death, to present you holy and unblameable and unreproveable in his sight.* (KJV)

Colossians 3:13 *Forbearing one another, and forgiving one another, if any man have a quarrel against any: even as Christ forgave you, so also do ye.* (KJV)

Ephesians 4:32 *And be ye kind one to another, tenderhearted, forgiving one another, even as God for Christ's sake hath forgiven you.* (KJV)

Romans 5:10 *For if, when we were enemies, we were reconciled to God by the death of his Son, much more, being reconciled, we shall be saved by his life.* (KJV)

2 Corinthians 5:18-21 *18 And all things are of God, who hath reconciled us to himself by Jesus Christ, and hath given to us the ministry of reconciliation; 19 To wit, that God was in Christ reconciling the world unto himself, not imputing their trespasses unto them; and hath committed unto us the word of reconciliation. 20 Now then we are ambassadors for Christ, as though God did beseech you by us: we pray you in Christ's stead, be ye reconciled to God. 21 For he hath made him to be sin for us, who knew no sin; that we might be made the righteousness of God in him.* (KJV)

PRAYER OF RECONCILIATION

Father God, in the name of Jesus. Thank you for pursuing us in our broken places. Thank you for desiring to reconcile us back to you and your love. You have never been swayed by our adultery or idolatry. There has never been a moment that you did not see the potential in our purpose. You are better to us than we could ever deserve. Thank you for not holding that over our heads but instead holding us in your arms. Thank you for continuing to draw us closer to you. Give us the heart to begin to draw close to you without prompting. Your love is enough. In Jesus' name, amen.

There has never been a moment that you did not see the potential in our purpose.

Day 2
Eyes on the Prize

LOT'S WIFE - THE WOMAN OF SALT

When you see "the woman of salt" I'm sure that there are a couple of scenarios that run through your mind. Someone that cried a lot. Or someone who was extremely petty or "salty". Someone who embodied the scripture "salt of the earth". Okay, so that was a bit deep, but you get the point.

Would you believe me if I told you that Lot's wife turned into an actual pillar of salt because she could not stay focused on the path before her? A LITERAL pillar of salt. That's the perfect example of when your mom says that you will reap a permanent consequence for scratching a temporary itch.

So, are you ready for one of the most profound lessons in being obedient? Let's read Genesis 19 together. Highlight verses 17 and 26. If you get nothing from today's story, hear this. When it is time to leave a place, pick up your feet and don't look back. There is nothing behind you that trumps where He is taking you. It doesn't matter how good, comfortable or familiar. Leave it. We can't become so attached to things, places or people. Especially when God is telling you that time is up.

Loves, when God tells you to do something there is always a reason. I want to encourage you to get over having to know why He's directing you to a certain path. Just go. He will never lead you into a situation that will leave you destitute. You have to learn to trust Him even when you don't understand His methods. He's guiding you to where you are meant to be so that you can take possession of what has always been yours.

But Lot's wife made the mistake of desiring what was not meant for her, more than she desired God. And we have all been there. We get comfortable in a season, relationship, job, mindset etc. and it becomes difficult for us to imagine anything else. We begin to unintentionally tether ourselves to things that have grown stale or even died. And that's dangerous because by tying ourselves to what is dead, we begin to die. There are no nutrients there and nothing that can sustain us. Friend, just because the Cinnamon Toast Crunch tastes good, that doesn't mean that the sugar won't make your teeth rot.

The angels of God were clear when they told Lot and his family to run and not look back. In fact, the angel told them that God planned to completely destroy the place where they lived. No one would be left but they would be saved. You wouldn't have to tell me twice! I am perfectly okay with removing myself from a toxic situation to get to a place that will restore my soul. We have to want better for ourselves than what society has told us is "achievement". We have to pursue divine purpose.

And let me give you this little nugget for free. The Word says that God would not destroy the cities if there was ONE who lived there who was worthy. There was not one. And that's clear because the angels confirmed that God had determined to destroy the area and all who dwelled there. That means Lot nor anyone in his family was worthy. But by grace, he was spared. If you think that God is blessing someone more than you, I encourage you to reevaluate your perspective. Grace is sometimes a teaching point, just as much as it is a blessing. Lot opened his home to the angels and in return, they created a window of opportunity for him to escape. It's not about what someone has that you don't have. It's about being thankful for the grace extended to each of us.

Lot's wife failed to see the grace offered to her and her family. Don't be like her. Be resolute in your decision to not only trust Him, but to follow Him.

AFFIRMATIONS

He will never lead me into the wilderness without a lamp.

What is behind me purposed me for what comes next.

Obedience will always be better than sacrifice.

SCRIPTURE BANK

Exodus 34:14 *For thou shalt worship no other god: for the Lord, whose name is Jealous, is a jealous God. (KJV)*

1 Samuel 15:22 *So Samuel said, "Has the Lord as great delight in burnt offerings and sacrifices, as in obeying the voice of the Lord? Behold, to obey is better than sacrifice, and to heed than the fat of rams. (NKJV)*

Philippians 4:9 *Those things, which ye have both learned, and received, and heard, and seen in me, do: and the God of peace shall be with you. (KJV)*

Isaiah 41:3 *He pursued them, and passed safely; even by the way that he had not gone with his feet. (KJV)*

Proverbs 3:5-6 **5** *Trust in the Lord with all thine heart; and lean not unto thine own understanding.* **6** *In all thy ways acknowledge him, and he shall direct thy paths. (KJV)*

Isaiah 41:10 *So do not fear, for I am with you; do not be dismayed, for I am your God. I will strengthen you and help you; I will uphold you with my righteous right hand. (NIV)*

Psalm 119:105 *Thy word is a lamp unto my feet, and a light unto my path. (KJV)*

Proverbs 3:5-6 *5 Trust in the Lord with all thine heart; and lean not unto thine own understanding. 6 In all thy ways acknowledge him, and he shall direct thy paths.* (KJV)

PRAYER OF RESOLUTION

Father God, in the name of Jesus. Thank you for building up our resolve. We have heard your Word and we believe your Word. Help us to apply it to our faith. Thank you for giving us the stamina to go the distance, no matter how far. We are ready to lean into you and your understanding. We know that our end is sure, keep reminding us to run and not allow our weariness to overtake us. Lord, thank you for grace and creating windows of opportunity that we do not deserve. Continue to use us for your glory and we will continue to go where you send us. In Jesus' name, amen.

We are ready to lean into you and your understanding.

Day 3
Don't Give Up the Pursuit

SHUNAMMITE WOMAN

When we focus on building the Kingdom and fulfilling our purpose, we have less time to think about what we don't have. It also creates the perfect opportunity for God to show us favor and meet our needs in a divine way. There's something about leaning into God and trusting His provision so much so, that we make intentional room for Him.

Let's read 2 Kings 4:8-36. I absolutely love the way that the Shunammite woman created space for the man of God and essentially God himself. She started by making sure that Elisha had food and a place to lay his head. Then when she realized that he would pass by her home often, she made a space specifically dedicated to him. How amazing would it be if we set aside space in our lives for God? A place that was all His own and occupied only by Him. I daresay that our relationship with Him would deepen and grow by leaps and bounds.

That's exactly what happened between the Shunammite woman and Elisha. She was so intentional in her care of him and his servant that he wanted to bless her in an extraordinary way. That's how God desires to bless us. In a way that can only be attributed to Him. He loves to pour blessings out lavishly. Just over the top blessings. Elisha went so far as to let her choose her gift. Yet she didn't articulate anything. She was content with where she was and what she had. Lesson? Learn contentment in this season so that you do not make your season of overflow an idol.

Gehazi knew that she had no children and her husband was elderly, so her chances to have a family were greatly reduced. But *she* did not ask for a baby. It was Elisha who told her that she would have a son the following year. The woman responded in a curious way by imploring Elisha not to toy with her heart. It seems that she had put to rest that desire and didn't want to be disappointed again. That's often how it is when we begin to seek God. We only ask for the things we think that He can "handle" and we tuck away those desires that mean the most. But God knew that by fulfilling her silent desire she would become an example of His glory manifested. Give Him space to expand your perspective of who He is.

Now let's fast forward.

When her son died, she pursued the prophet even though it wasn't a holy day or a new month. It didn't matter to her what anyone, including her husband, thought about her ditching protocol. She was focused on pursuing the one who could help. And she didn't stop until she reached him. And while her journey is important, it is her adamant refusal to leave his presence without receiving what she came for that is game-changing. When we pursue God, we must have the mentality that we will receive an impartation each time. There should never be a time that we leave His presence without a fresh anointing when we have actively pursued Him. Never.

But my favorite part is in verse 30. Elisha left where he was and traveled to where she needed him. God does the exact same thing. If we pursue Him and get into the posture of transparency, He will meet us where we need Him. Every. Single. Time.

Don't give up the pursuit, loves.

AFFIRMATIONS

He will meet all of my needs. Spoken and unspoken.

He is making room for me.

He will come to where I am.

SCRIPTURE BANK

Philippians 4:12-13 *12 I know both how to make do with little, and I know how to make do with a lot. In any and all circumstances I have learned the secret of being content—whether well fed or hungry, whether in abundance or in need. 13 I am able to do all things through him who strengthens me. (CSB)*

2 Kings 4:30 *And the mother of the child said, As the Lord liveth, and as thy soul liveth, I will not leave thee. And he arose, and followed her. (KJV)*

Matthew 18:18-19 *18 Verily I say unto you, Whatsoever ye shall bind on earth shall be bound in heaven: and whatsoever ye shall loose on earth shall be loosed in heaven. 19 Again I say unto you, That if two of you shall agree on earth as touching any thing that they shall ask, it shall be done for them of my Father which is in heaven. (KJV)*

Joshua 1:9 *Have not I commanded thee? Be strong and of a good courage; be not afraid, neither be thou dismayed: for the Lord thy God is with thee whithersoever thou goest. (KJV)*

Psalm 91:1-2 *1 He that dwelleth in the secret place of the most High shall abide under the shadow of the Almighty. 2 I will say of the Lord, He is my refuge and my fortress: my God; in Him will I trust. (KJV)*

Psalm 112:6-8 *6 Surely he shall not be moved forever: the righteous shall be in everlasting remembrance. 7 He shall not be afraid of evil tidings: his heart is fixed, trusting in the Lord.* ***8*** *His heart is established, he shall not be afraid, until he see his desire upon his enemies. (KJV)*

PRAYER OF EXPANSION

Father God, in the name of Jesus. Thank you for an opportunity to show you deference. Thank you for an opportunity to be in direct communion with you and to have you in our space. Thank you for passing by more than once, giving us multiple chances to sit at your feet and learn. We are committed to making room for you in our daily lives. We will set aside space and time that is solely dedicated to you and your rest. Thank you for dwelling in our temples. Lord, thank you for recognizing our need to expand our mindset. You want to bless us; we just have to make room for the blessing. In Jesus' name, amen.

*He will meet all of my needs.
Spoken and unspoken.*

Day 4
Pre-Planned

MANOAH'S WIFE

Have you ever had an occasion to see God and know without a shadow of a doubt that it was God? You just know that the situation would have taken you out *but for* Him?

Judges 13 tells the story of Samson's miraculous conception. His mother was barren, but God used her desert place as the stage for redemption for God's people. For people who had willingly turned from Him. Take comfort in that. Even when we have run so far from God, He is actively pursuing us. He is already mapping out a path of return or a plan to rescue us. He loves us so much. So much more than we can comprehend.

And one of the ways that He shows His love for us is by giving us specific rules and boundaries.

An example of this is when an angel of the Lord showed himself to Manoah's wife and gave her very specific instructions. These instructions helped to set in motion that Samson was set apart and consecrated for the great work of God. By being clear with her that she would need to cut out anything considered unclean, He made it possible for His spirit to take root in her. God can't dwell in an unclean place, folks!

But, let's get back to what I want us to focus on from this story. Verses 19 through 23. God is preparing to show you things and completely turn the status quo on its head. It's probably going to terrify you how impossibly amazing He is. Just know that He is not taking you through this season right now for nothing. He wouldn't have mapped out such an intentional plan, if He didn't have a distinct purpose for you. Don't get distracted or discouraged as you wait on Him to come through. Your sacrifice and your discomfort are not in vain. In fact, through your loss He has more room to bless you.

Manoah's wife recognized that God had a divine purpose for her all along. What had appeared to be her barren season was a dormant harvest. God had cleared the field (she was barren), he had prepared the field (instructions for during her pregnancy), sowed the seed (opened her husband's eyes to God), watered the seed (gave them peace about His divinity) and grew the harvest (the birth of Samson).

There is a plan in place that was divinely created for you. You just have to pursue it. No matter how long it takes or how difficult it is for other people to understand. Keep going.

AFFIRMATIONS

He desires to show me His glory.

I could have been dead, but God's purpose prevailed.

You knew me from the beginning and loved me.

SCRIPTURE BANK

Psalm 139:13-16 *13 For thou hast possessed my reins: thou hast covered me in my mother's womb. 14 I will praise thee; for I am fearfully and wonderfully made: marvelous are thy works; and that my soul knoweth right well. 15 My substance was not hid from thee, when I was made in secret, and curiously wrought in the lowest parts of the earth.* **16** *Thine eyes did see my substance, yet being imperfect; and in thy book all my members were written, which in continuance were fashioned, when as yet there was none of them. (KJV)*

Ephesians 1:4 *According as he hath chosen us in him before the foundation of the world, that we should be holy and without blame before him in love. (KJV)*

Isaiah 44:2 *Thus saith the Lord that made thee, and formed thee from the womb, which will help thee; Fear not, O Jacob, my servant; and thou, Jesurun, whom I have chosen. (KJV)*

Jeremiah 1:5 *Before I formed thee in the belly I knew thee; and before thou camest forth out of the womb I sanctified thee, and I ordained thee a prophet unto the nations. (KJV)*

Romans 8:29 *For whom he did foreknow, he also did predestinate to be conformed to the image of his Son, that he might be the firstborn among many brethren. (KJV)*

PRAYER OF SIGHT

Lord, thank you. You have opened our eyes to the realization of your glory. Thank you for the plan that has always been outlined for our lives. Even in our darkest place, you saw purpose. Thank you for showing us how to properly love you through our obedience. Train our eyes to find you in every situation and to focus on you. When things become fuzzy, blaze a trail. We want to see you and know you. In Jesus' name, amen.

Day 5
Pursuit of Faith

LOIS AND EUNICE

When I think about my children, I also think about the legacy that I am leaving them. Not money or houses… but a legacy of faith. How beautiful would it be for my children to become adults and have a foundation of faith as they pursue a personal relationship with Christ?

In 2 Timothy 1, Paul celebrated the strong faith of Timothy and thanked God for Timothy's resolve to trust God in all things. A trait that was handed down by his grandmother, Lois, and his mother, Eunice.

2 Timothy 1:5 is the only verse where these women are mentioned and yet it gives us a powerful glimpse of their character. They were followers of God and instilled a strong sense of faith in young Timothy. Paul constantly talks about all that Timothy had learned and put into practice and it stands to reason that some of that learning took place at the hands of Lois and Eunice.

We must pursue faith every chance we get. We must actively seek out opportunities to grow our trust of the character of God. These two women had to be mighty powerhouses of faith because Timothy's father and grandfather are not mentioned. Just Lois and Eunice. They left an indelible mark on him that would help him to stay the course until the very end.

We don't have to have a monument erected in our honor. We just need for our legacy to be the faith we lived by. Timothy is known as a man of faith because of the women who raised him to be one.

What will your circle of influence say about you when you have left the room? Whose life will turn to Christ because of your commitment to stay the course? What glory will be manifested because of your faith?

Pursue a life of faith and the rest will figure itself out.

AFFIRMATIONS

My faith can move mountains.

My faith will impact a generation.

My family will be game changers for Christ.

SCRIPTURE BANK

Matthew 8:10 *Hearing this, Jesus was amazed and said to those following Him, "Truly I tell you, I have not found anyone in Israel with so great a faith." (NIV)*

Matthew 19:26 *But Jesus beheld them, and said unto them, With men this is impossible; but with God all things are possible. (KJV)*

1 Peter 5:7 *Casting all your care upon him; for he careth for you. (KJV)*

Mark 12:30 *And thou shalt love the Lord thy God with all thy heart, and with all thy soul, and with all thy mind, and with all thy strength: this is the first commandment. (KJV)*

Luke 12:25-26 **25** *Can any of you add one moment to his life span by worrying?* **26** *If then, you're not able to do even a little thing, why worry about the rest? (CSB)*

Ephesians 3:16 *That he would grant you, according to the riches of his glory, to be strengthened with might by his Spirit in the inner man. (NKJV)*

Habakkuk 3:19 *The Lord God is my strength, and he will make my feet like hinds' feet, and he will make me to walk upon mine high places. To the chief singer on my stringed instruments. (KJV)*

Proverbs 18:10 *The name of the Lord is a strong tower: the righteous runneth into it and is safe. (KJV)*

PRAYER OF FAITH

Father God, in the name of Jesus. Thank you for peace and for covering. Thank you for this opportunity to grow and to see our faith put into action as we follow you out into the deep. Call us and we will come. Father, you know everything that we have need of. We rest in that knowledge so that we can focus on bringing you glory. Our faith knows no limits and your provision has no bounds. Grow our faith so that it may have roots like Lois and Eunice. Thank you for being worthy of our praise, honor and trust. In Jesus' name, amen.

Call us and we will come.

Week Four Exercise

For our last exercise, I want you to write down your personal prayer of faith. Share with God your desire to pursue and be pursued. Thank Him for what He has done and what He has kept you from. Write whatever comes to mind! It's okay if you are hurting or angry... share that with Him. But then allow Him to give you the joy He has always meant for you to have. It is time for you to be transparent about your process and where you are in it.

Once you have written it down, I want you to go put it in a safe place. A place that shows honor. I want you to begin to cherish your transparent relationship with God and your honest pursuit of MORE. When you feel alone or heavy, go and take it out and remember that He wants to sit with you, wherever you are. And not only will He sit with you, but He will take on your burdens as if they are His own. He loves you that much.

For the second part of your assignment, I want you to identify an accountability partner if you don't already have one. When training for a marathon, it's always beneficial to have someone supporting you along the way. Same concept. Your accountability partner should be someone that you are comfortable being transparent with, that you respect their counsel, that will support you in your growth and encourage you to re-evaluate poor habits. You are gearing up for the race of a lifetime. Get a running mate.

God has always desired to demonstrate His love and care for you. All that He asks, is that you trust His process. The manifestation of reaching your #faithgoals will be worth it.

The manifestation of reaching your #faithgoals will be worth it.

EPILOGUE

This has been an incredible journey of identifying the different levels of faith and the joy found within the process. That joy comes from trusting Him, realizing our purpose and pushing forward when it's tough. Our daily goal should be to exponentially increase our faith through constant communion with Him.

My prayer is that over these four weeks, you have begun to identify the weak areas in your faith and committed to strengthening them. What He has planned for you is far greater than any discomfort or pain you will experience along the way. It is time that we activate our faith and begin to experience the fullness of His joy. We cannot get overwhelmed by the tests of our faith. We must actively pursue the joy of fulfilling our purpose…We were created to bring Him glory and that is an honor.

#FaithGoals Romans 8:18

I consider that our present sufferings are not worth comparing with the glory that will be revealed in us. (NIV)

ABOUT THE AUTHOR

Petra Michele Pindar is an attorney, worship leader, speaker and author. She is passionate about the call that God has placed on her heart to encourage women of all ages to seek Christ in their everyday connections and interactions. Petra is an avid believer in the power of friendship and how it can strengthen the discipline of faith. As the founder of "A Few Good Thoughts" ministry based on Philippians 4:8, she promotes active discipleship through godly friendships and connections that focus on positive thoughts and encouragement. Petra follows the example of Christ, who surrounded himself with like-minded individuals to pursue His greatest calling and effect the world for change.

She is happily married to her "once in a lifetime" Robert Pindar and together, they are the parents to Jackson Gray and Sterling Lewis. It is her greatest honor to serve in this, her first ministry, with excellence. God has truly blessed her beyond her wildest dreams to be surrounded by her favorite guys.

Petra would love for you to connect with her on Instagram or Facebook @PetraPindar and join her tribe of women pursuing godly friendships and intentional connection with Christ. Be sure to subscribe to www.petrapindar.com to check out what's happening with A Few Good Thoughts and to join her online outreach group, TRIBE.

www.ingramcontent.com/pod-product-compliance
Lightning Source LLC
Chambersburg PA
CBHW040455240426
43663CB00033B/12